Strong Local Leadership – Quality Publi

Cm 5327

ISBN 0 10 153272 5

CORRECTION

Part II, Chapter 9, Paragraph 9.14 (page 126)

There is a minor typographical error in line 4 where "over" should read "under".
Once corrected, this paragraph will therefore read (the corrected text is highlighted in
bold):

"9.14   The Audit Commission recently published a paper 'A New Approach to Local Council Audit',
which outlines the new audit regime due to be launched in early 2002 in time for the 2001-02
audit round. This essentially makes the audit process much simpler and therefore much cheaper.
Under the new regime, parishes with either receipts or payments of **under** £100,000 per year
will be subject to a 'basic' audit which entails a large amount of self-certification and an
analytical review by the auditor based on the paperwork presented. It is estimated that the
smallest parishes - below £5,000 - will have audit fees of £30-£50 – a saving of about £100 on
the current average cost. Parishes at the £50,000 – 100,000 level will be charged £250 – £350 –
saving roughly £200 on the average cost. Parishes falling between £100,000 and £500,000 will
be subjected to an 'intermediate' audit and should see savings of approximately 12 per cent on
current costs. Best value parishes will still be subject to a full audit and may see an increase
(about 9 per cent). The Commission's view is that the triennial audit scheme will become
redundant under this approach and they estimate that 90 per cent of parishes currently on the
triennial scheme should have savings in costs under the new regime."

December 2001
LONDON: THE STATIONERY OFFICE

Strong Local Leadership – Quality Public Services

Presented to Parliament by the Secretary of State for Transport,
Local Government and the Regions,
by Command of Her Majesty.
December 2001

CM5327

£18.75

The DTLR has actively considered the needs of the partially sighted in accessing this white paper. The text will be made available in full at **http://www.local-regions.dtlr.gov.uk/index.htm** in full accordance with W3C Web Accessiblity Initiative's criteria. The text may be freely downloaded by individuals or organisations for conversion or translation into other accessible formats.

Department for Transport, Local Government and the Regions
Eland House
Bressenden Place
London SW1E 5DU
Telephone 020 7944 3000
Web site www.dtlr.gov.uk

December 2001

Foreword

This white paper sets out a new vision for local government at the beginning of the 21st Century. It seeks to establish a partnership between central and local government, reflecting the critical importance of local authorities as a tier of democratic government, delivering high quality public services to local people.

Democratically-elected councils are part of the fabric of our communities. The services they provide have a vital part to play in sustaining and enhancing the social and economic prospects and environmental quality of our towns, cities and countryside. They can have a profound effect on the opportunities and quality of life of the people who live and work there.

People want good standards of education, safe communities, efficient transport systems and high quality care for the vulnerable in our society. They want clean streets, decent housing, good leisure and cultural facilities, and well-planned neighbourhoods. They want their voices to be heard when decisions are made about how these services are delivered, and they want someone looking after and speaking up for the interests of their communities.

People therefore expect a great deal from their council. And those expectations are rising. To meet them, councils have constantly to seek new and more effective ways to deliver customer-focused services and lead their communities. The proposals in this white paper will provide a framework in which all can do so, through the application of the Government's four principles of public services reform:

Establishing a **national framework of standards and accountability** for the delivery of high quality services and effective community leadership

Within this framework, **devolution to local councils to encourage diversity and creativity**, giving them the freedom they need to respond to and meet their communities' needs.

Building local capacity in recognition of the need for **flexibility at the front-line** to exploit the opportunities we are opening up, and deliver the improved services and effective leadership we all want to see.

And more **choice for customers**, with access to an alternative supplier where performance falls below acceptable standards.

The implementation of this white paper will see greater freedoms for high performing councils, incentives to support the achievement of stretching targets, focused attention where councils are struggling, and effective intervention to tackle failure.

These proposals form part of the Government's agenda for modernisation and reform. For many, they will be challenging. They are meant to be. We propose these changes not for their own sake, but because local people will benefit. From the requirement that all services should be delivered to an acceptable standard. From the fact that the changes we all really want to see – better schools and social care, improved local environments, better transport and other vital local services – will get the priority they deserve. And from effective community leadership by councils in touch with local people and working to meet their aspirations.

I want to see central and local government working together in a constructive partnership to deliver the high quality public services that local people have the right to expect. In a practical way this white paper shows how we can do so.

Tony Blair

Tony Blair

CONTENTS

CONTENTS: PART I

CHAPTER 1
Introduction

We want a vibrant local democracy in which councils deliver high quality and improving local services and provide strong and confident leadership.

We will work with local government to achieve this and remove unnecessary controls which stifle local innovation. The proposals we set out in this white paper mark a radical change in the relationship between central and local government.

Strengthening local government

1.1.　The Government wants to see strong, vibrant, innovative and responsive local government delivering the quality of local leadership and public services that their communities need. Councils are run by people elected by the local community. That gives them a unique role and responsibility to respond to local needs and circumstances, and to provide the leadership that helps to create and support thriving communities.

1.2.　The proof that they can do so is all around us. In the magnificent municipal achievements of the nineteenth century. In the contribution that councils made to the establishment of our welfare system and economic prosperity in the last century. And it is there today in the things which councils up and down the country do day in and day out to help make peoples' lives better.

1.3.　Four years ago councils were not well placed to respond to the Government's vision of successful local government. The resources they needed for essential investment were not in place. An effective, constructive partnership between central and local government did not exist. Universal capping and compulsory competitive tendering (CCT) were the order of the day, focusing on inputs and relegating the achievement of outcomes that matter, such as

improvements in education, social care, housing and transport, and the creation of a clean and safe local environment.

1.4.　Since 1997 the Government has introduced a wide range of measures designed to develop better local leadership and focus on service delivery. Financial support for councils' revenue and capital expenditure has risen in real terms in each of the last four years (in stark contrast to the 4 years before that), alongside financial reforms including the end of universal capping.

1.5.　A major public service reform programme has begun. The bureaucracy of CCT has gone. In its place, councils strive for continuous improvement through the achievement of best value. This means balancing costs and quality in consultation with local people, and identifying the most appropriate method of service delivery, be it public, private, voluntary, or in partnership. Local Public Service Agreements (PSAs) encourage councils to stretch their performance still further, in return for additional finance and the freedoms and flexibilities needed to do so.

1.6.　The new constitutions that councils are introducing following consultation with local people will improve the efficiency, transparency and accountability of local leadership and decision making. The introduction of statutory community strategies and the broad new enabling power to promote community well-being encourage councils to face outwards and work alongside public, private and voluntary partners to develop and deliver their communities' vision for their locality.

1.7. We need to build on these reforms to ensure effective service delivery and community leadership across the whole of local government. Further reform is needed so that councils have the tools they need to make the improvements local people want to see. In particular, we need to get rid of regulations where these impede councils in finding innovative ways of tackling local problems, and to modernise local government finance.

1.8. Reform is needed because Government has a responsibility to ensure that wherever people live in this country, they have access to good quality public services. Where local government is responsible for providing these services, it must be held to account for achieving appropriate standards across the country. That means tackling the current variability in service quality, especially in critical areas like education and social services.

1.9. Reform is needed to lay the foundations for local government's future. A future in which councils enjoy the confidence of all the partners they work with and all the people they serve, and which sees local government return to the very centre of life in their communities.

1.10. The proposals we set out here will mark a new and lasting basis for effective local government – by celebrating councils as a significant and vital sphere of government and by enhancing their ability to make a real difference to peoples' lives.

Summary of proposals

1.11 We will support councils to make a success of their unique role as democratically-elected leaders of their local communities. We will help them to develop the democratic legitimacy and sound governance needed to underpin community leadership and effective service delivery building on the new well-being powers and local strategic partnerships. We will encourage other public sector partners to work effectively with councils to tackle local problems and exploit local opportunities. We will promote closer engagement between councils and their communities, and give councils further powers to serve local people and improve the local environment and public spaces. We will allow councils to introduce Business Improvement Districts to promote partnership with local businesses. Significant deregulation will increase councils' freedom of action.

1.12 In line with our principles for public service reform, we will shift our focus to the assured delivery of outcomes through a national framework of standards and accountability, and away from controls over inputs, processes and local decisions. This white paper sets out a comprehensive performance framework for improvement, accompanied by a substantial package of deregulation.

1.13 The framework (which will be complemented by the new performance rating system for social services) comprises:

- clearly defined priorities and exacting performance standards, developed with local government through the Central Local Partnership;

- regular comprehensive performance assessments for all councils, identifying how they are performing against these standards;

- co-ordinated incentives, rewards and tools which address the results of the comprehensive assessments and drive service improvement including:

  – clear and concise public information about councils' performance;

– integrated inspection programmes tailored to councils' strengths, weaknesses and needs;

– additional freedoms, powers and flexibility over resources for councils with the track-record and capacity to use them;

– tough action to tackle failing councils and services;

– stretching targets and rewards for service improvement, through local PSAs; and

– a streamlined, proportionate and integrated best value regime.

1.14   With this framework in place there will be an increased emphasis on delivery, responsibility and accountability. By removing restrictions and requirements on planning, spending and decision-making and providing new powers to trade and charge, we will free up councils to innovate and deliver tangible improvements in the quality of services and effective community leadership. Unnecessary bureaucracy, red-tape and regulation will be removed for all councils. We will adopt a more co-ordinated and proportionate approach to the demands we make of councils, focusing on the delivery of priorities and outcomes. There will be more financial freedom within a basic framework underpinned by sound financial management and prudent decision-making.

1.15   Specifically, for all councils we will:

• abolish the council tax benefit subsidy limitation scheme;

• shift control over council borrowing decisions to the local level;

• significantly reduce the numbers of plans and strategies that councils are required to produce;

• scale back on area-based initiatives and give greater scope to rationalise partnerships;

• remove unnecessary red tape and bureaucracy including many requirements for councils to obtain Government consent before acting;

• provide councils with wider powers to provide services to others; and

• allow councils to charge for the discretionary services they provide.

1.16   Additional freedoms will be available for high performers, with less ring-fencing, fewer planning requirements and greater freedom to use income from fines. These councils will also have more discretion over best value reviews, a much lighter touch inspection regime and the widest freedom to trade across their services. We will not use reserve powers to cap the council tax increases of high performing councils. Other councils will also be able to agree additional freedoms, depending on their performance profile. Freedoms will also be negotiable through local PSAs, to accelerate progress on key national and local priorities.

1.17   This package of reforms demonstrates Government's commitment to bring about vibrant, innovative and responsive local government. Local authorities will have more freedom and responsibility to improve their performance and serve their communities. This will enhance local democracy, with local authorities being more clearly accountable to their electorate for service delivery and council tax levels. In return, Government will expect local authorities to rise to the challenge and bring about significant improvements in performance and overall efficiency.

1.18   Police authorities are a special type of local authority, whose national standards and priorities are the responsibility of the Home Secretary. They will retain their own separate performance framework and will benefit from elements of the wider local authority proposals, such as the new freedom to borrow.

1.19   We will draw together support, on a cross-departmental basis, for:

- building councils' capacity to deliver; and

- improving the skills of councillors and council staff.

1.20   The emphasis will be on targeting resources where they are needed most and on enabling councils themselves to tackle their weaknesses and develop their strengths. Chapter 5 seeks views on our proposals to do this. We will help councils to exploit the potential that new technologies offer to restructure services, speed up transactions, provide a single point of contact for people's needs and join up delivery by local authorities and other agencies.

1.21   We will promote sound financial management in local government including requiring councils to maintain adequate reserves and keep finances under review. We will reform the single capital pot to reduce the proportion of ring-fencing of Government support for capital investment for high performing and striving councils.

1.22   Chapter 6 outlines our proposals for reform of the local government finance system including reforms for parish and town councils. Part II of this publication describes our local government finance proposals in detail.

1.23   We will clarify accountability for financial decisions. In providing greater responsibility to councils for decisions on borrowing, fees and charges and council tax, we will also strengthen the scrutiny role of councillors and reinforce the need for local consultation. Council tax bills will be clearer. They will show the annual percentage change in council tax for different authorities up front, not hidden away in a leaflet.

1.24   We will design new grant formulae that are more intelligible and transparent to all stakeholders.

1.25   The Government's goals of bringing decisions closer to the people they affect, increasing democratic participation and improving the efficiency and effectiveness of service delivery are also being addressed at a regional level. The Government is committed to publishing a white paper setting out proposals for giving people in the English regions a better say in how they are governed. These proposals will be based on the drawing down of powers from central government, as part of our wider commitment to devolution. This will have close links with the ways in which we are strengthening the role of local government and improving the working relationships between different levels of governance.

Wales

1.26   The policy proposals set out in this white paper are for England. The National Assembly for Wales will be consulting shortly on proposals for local government in Wales.

CHAPTER 2
Leading and empowering communities

An effective local democracy, with strong and accountable political leadership, is central to community leadership and the delivery of public services.

We will support councils in their efforts to lead their communities and meet people's needs. In particular we will:

- help councils to enhance their democratic legitimacy and improve governance;

- encourage other public sector bodies to work effectively with councils;

- support greater levels of community engagement and involvement in council business;

- give councils greater freedom and more powers to meet people's needs; and

- allow the introduction of Business Improvement Districts.

Why local democratic leadership matters

2.1   Thriving communities and strong democratic leadership go hand in hand. Such leadership helps to enhance the quality of life of individuals and communities, boost the local economy, improve the environment, and contribute to the achievement of wider regional and national policy goals. Councils are uniquely placed to provide this leadership. The Government is committed to helping them to do so.

THE VALUE OF DEMOCRATIC ACCOUNTABILITY

2.2   Effective local democracy is essential to strong community leadership and improved service delivery. Because they are elected by their communities, councillors play a unique role in linking the delivery of services with local people's needs and ambitions.

2.3   Resources are finite, and communities' views and priorities can diverge and conflict. Consensus cannot always be reached, and so choices and compromises have to be made. That can mean creating winners and losers, trading short-term losses for long-term gains, or foregoing one set of opportunities in order to exploit another. It also means making strategic choices for future generations not just dealing with immediate interests and issues. Democratically-elected councils provide the means for expressing and resolving these conflicts, for ensuring that differing points of view are heard and understood, for promoting understanding, and for making tough choices. Councils are then responsible for explaining those choices and will be held to account for them by local people.

2.4   Councils – unlike any other local organisation – are designed specifically to play this role.

COMMUNITY COHESION AND CIVIC RENEWAL

2.5   Communities and places differ and change, and so do the challenges they face. Local areas are becoming more diverse. Our towns, cities and rural areas contain many communities, often sharing space and resources, with many similarities but also significant differences.

2.6   Communities everywhere face rapid changes to their economy, environment and social mix. The leaders of those communities have to adapt continually to such changes. The best councils anticipate change and respond accordingly. Shifts in economic activity are met by developing new foundations on which to build economic success. Changes in cultural mix are met by developing positive community relations and promoting inclusiveness. Failures in community leadership can contribute to a breakdown in community cohesion. This can lead in the most serious cases to the sorts of incidents of civil disorder that we saw last summer in a small number of our towns and cities. A report on these incidents produced by the Ministerial Group on Public Order and Community Cohesion[1] examines the link between community leadership and community cohesion in more detail.

2.7   Successful councils ensure that the voices of all get heard – not just the most vociferous, powerful or well-established. They assess the problems faced by different groups and tackle discrimination and disadvantage wherever it is found. They enable individuals, families and communities to find and develop solutions to their own problems, provide the resources and opportunities to help them do so, and work with others to contribute to those solutions. They stand up and speak out for all local people. And they engage them in the design and delivery of services.

DELIVERING SUSTAINABLE DEVELOPMENT

2.8   Strong community leadership means providing the economic infrastructure needed by local businesses to compete successfully on the local, regional or wider stage. It means developing social capital by supporting civic engagement and networks of neighbourhood organisations. It means enhancing environmental quality by reducing waste, energy use and air pollution and improving public

space. And it means safeguarding the interests of future members of the community. Many decisions made now will have long term implications. These need to be identified, understood and designed into local policies. These are not separate goals – sustainable development means addressing all of them at the same time.

2.9   Communities are inter-dependent. Actions taken at sub-regional or regional level can have a profound effect on the development of local areas. Local activity contributes to the achievement of wider goals. Someone needs to champion their communities' interests at these wider levels, join up with neighbouring areas to identify and achieve common goals and take local action which promotes the wider economic or environmental interests of the region and beyond. Councils are the best placed local bodies to do this.

DELIVERING HIGH QUALITY SERVICES

2.10   The Government believes that all residents, no matter where they live, are entitled to good quality public services. Local government has a key role to play in enabling people to receive this entitlement, through arrangements that reflect local circumstances and that empower local communities. This is particularly true of services (such as social services, planning, transport and leisure) that need to be tailored to the particular needs of the locality or individual service users. And it is true for problems which are to some extent rooted in local circumstances and therefore vary from area to area (neighbourhood renewal and improving public spaces are good examples). Local authorities are well placed to achieve this balance between national policy goals and local service delivery.

---

[1] This report is to be published by the Home Office shortly.

A ROLE FOR ALL COUNCILS

2.11 All councils can contribute to effective democratic leadership. As the most local form of democratic governance, parish and town councils have an invaluable role to play in identifying needs in rural areas and market towns, and then working with others to meet them. Our proposals to establish Quality Parishes[2] will strengthen their role still further.

2.12 Districts have a strong local presence too. They are responsible for many of the services – planning, housing, leisure, environmental services – which have a direct impact on quality of life. The contribution of upper-tier authorities, especially for education and social services, is equally important. This is the level at which links to other key service deliverers – such as the health service and the police – can most effectively be formed.

2.13 Each tier therefore makes an important and distinctive contribution. Effective working between all tiers – both strategically through local partnerships and in the day to day delivery of services – is essential if communities are to be well-served by their councils.

Helping councils to lead their communities

2.14 Responsibility for community leadership rests with councils. Government can help to create the conditions that enable councils to make a success of their leadership role. As Government at all levels must recognise, real

leadership has to be earned – it cannot be conferred through the ballot box alone. To be successful community leaders, councils need:

- democratic legitimacy;
- sound governance;
- effective partnerships with other local organisations and their communities;
- powers that enable them to make a real difference;
- real community engagement and empowerment;
- room to respond effectively to local priorities;
- continuous improvement in their service delivery; and
- a willingness to exploit the potential afforded by new technologies.

2.15 The Government has already taken action to help councils with each of these. We can and will do more.

DEMOCRATIC LEGITIMACY

2.16 Improving turnout is one of the key ways of bolstering democratic legitimacy and civic engagement. Currently, turnout at elections is falling and in local elections is frequently below 35%. There are many reasons for this. Reversing the trend will require long term changes in people's behaviour. In their report on the 2001 elections[3] the Electoral Commission concluded that it is above all the quality and persuasiveness of policies put forward by the political parties

---

2 *Our Countryside: The Future A Fair Deal for Rural England,* DETR, MAFF, November 2000, Cm 4909, ISBN 0101490925.
http://www.defra.gov.uk/erdp/erdpfrm.htm
Quality Parish and Town Councils: A Consultation Paper, DEFRA, DTLR, NALC, LGA, Countryside Agency, November 2001
http://www.defra.gov.uk/wildlife-countryside/consult/qtpc/index.htm

3 *Election 2001: The Official Results* Electoral Commission, Politico's Publishing, July 2001, ISBN 1842750208.
http://www.electoralcommission.gov.uk/publications.htm

and their ability to motivate voters that will determine future trends for electoral turnout. This is as true for local elections as for Parliamentary elections. The Commission recognise also that it is essential to modernise electoral arrangements and respond to people's changing expectations.

2.17 Central and local government have a shared interest in working with the Commission to tackle these issues. We will continue with pilots of electoral innovations, including investing in and promoting e-voting. We are working with the Improvement and Development Agency (IDeA), local government and others to introduce an electronic register of electors. And we are developing an implementation plan and strategy for e-democracy and e-voting.

2.18 The current cycle of local government elections is confusing. Some councils have elections once every four years while others have elections in three years out of four. It is too easy for electors to lose track of when elections are to be held or how many votes they have on any particular election day. And this arrangement can lessen the immediate impact of voters' behaviour on council control. We will therefore invite the Electoral Commission to propose options to simplify the current cycle of local elections.

SOUND GOVERNANCE

2.19 People will have more confidence in their councils as leaders if they know who actually makes the decisions, how they are made, and how the decision-makers are held to account.

2.20 Our approach is that people should be able to choose how they are governed locally. Councils need to listen to people's views when deciding what their constitutions should be and how to conduct their business. The reforms introduced in last year's Local Government Act provide a range of choices. Decisions will be made efficiently and openly by people who are visible to their communities, and overview and scrutiny arrangements will strengthen the links between councillors and the people they represent.

2.21 We have introduced statutory codes of conduct, standards committees, and the independent Standards Board for England. This framework means that councils operate under a more rigorous ethical regime than any other local partner. These measures will help to halt the slide in public trust caused by the small number of high-profile cases of councillor misconduct.

2.22 To support these changes, we will

- work with the Local Government Association (LGA) and the IDeA to develop a best practice programme on how the new arrangements are operating;

- evaluate the benefits that new constitutions are bringing, and ensure the results inform the work that councils do;

- review the help and guidance we give to local authorities;

- support efforts by the IDeA and others to build capacity for political leadership; and

- continue to support local authorities in developing their approach to overview and scrutiny. We will clarify our statutory guidance to make clear our view that overview and scrutiny committees should:

    – focus on reviewing the actual outcomes that their councils' policies are achieving for local people in practice, as well as reviewing the policies themselves;

    – search for innovative ways to improve the quality of services within best value;

    – involve other local stakeholders in their work; and

    – review the work of other local service providers.

2.23 We are monitoring the experience of those councils who have held referendums and are now moving forward to hold elections for a mayor. In last year's Urban White Paper we said that where local people think that a directly elected mayor is right for their town or city, they should have the opportunity to vote for one.

2.24 In partnership with councils where people have decided to pursue this form of governance, we will develop a support programme which includes:

- education of voters about mayors and the voting system;

- learning from the lessons of the first round of mayoral referendums and elections, in order to refine and improve the process, in particular how people go about submitting a petition to require a referendum; and

- sharing information with all councils on best practice.

2.25 As experience grows, we want councils to look again at their constitutions, including the form of leadership chosen, taking account of local opinion. We therefore propose that after a set period – perhaps five years – councils should review their constitutions. Local choice will remain the guiding principle, based on full consultation and, where appropriate, referendums.

2.26 Councils will need to bring to such reviews the developing body of best practice and the experience of others. We will help local authorities to undertake such reviews and look to see that they are guided by what local people tell them. We believe that independent and representative democracy commissions provide a good vehicle for this.

2.27 We recognise that there are circumstances where having a mayor would have particular benefits, for example where a council has been failing and requires decisive managerial and political leadership to sustain improvement. In chapter 3 we set out proposals for intervening in failing councils. One option would involve putting the council into a form of administration for an interim period. As the position stabilised following this, we think that, subject to the views of local people in a referendum, a mayor and council manager could provide the decisive leadership to ensure that improvement is sustained. We will set out more detailed proposals on this in due course.

2.28 It is important that local authorities continue to operate transparently and increase the openness with which they do business. Authorities already operating executive arrangements must publish a forward plan containing details of key decisions they are going to take and they must take such collective decisions in public. We have defined key decisions as those which will result in significant savings or expenditure or which are likely to have a significant impact on two or more electoral divisions or wards within the local authority, or both.

2.29 Following consultation,[4] we believe local authorities are best placed to make the choice as to what constitutes a key decision for this purpose. We plan to review the access to information regime for councils during 2002 at the same time as we are preparing for implementation of the Freedom of Information Act in local government. As part of this, we will work with authorities and the LGA to identify best practice in defining what is a key decision.

---

[4] *Access to Information in Local Government: A Consultation Paper on Aspects of the Access to Information Regime for Local Authorities in England*, DETR, April 2001 http://www.local-regions.detr.gov.uk/consult/infoinlg/index.htm

EFFECTIVE PARTNERSHIPS

2.30   In recent years there has been an increasing recognition, in both central and local government, of the importance of successful partnership working. To tackle our most challenging problems – on health, crime, education, transport, housing and the local environment – we need to marshal the contributions of the public, private and voluntary sectors, and of communities themselves. We will not achieve genuinely citizen-centred services unless service deliverers work well together.

2.31   The Government has done a great deal to encourage such partnerships in policy and service delivery at both national and local levels. We are committed to building on the successful track record of partnerships like the New Commitment to Regeneration and Health Action Zones. In particular, we will complete our drive to establish effective local strategic partnerships (LSPs). These partnerships are the key element in developing integrated approaches to local service delivery, and to tackling policy priorities in a joined-up way. They bring together service deliverers, communities, the voluntary sector and business to identify local priorities and to devise and implement strategies to meet them. They also lead local efforts to close the gap in living standards and opportunities between the most deprived neighbourhoods and other areas.

2.32   We are therefore committed to playing our part to help LSPs succeed. Local authorities and their partners have put in a great deal of effort to establish LSPs. In many areas, significant progress has been made, and examples of exciting and genuinely inclusive approaches to partnership working are beginning to emerge.

2.33   In practice, it is clear that success depends on securing the effective involvement of the public, private, voluntary and community sectors. Local partners are best placed to decide how to achieve this. So the detailed structure, membership, and geographical coverage of LSPs should be determined locally.

2.34   The Government Office accreditation process now underway in the 88 most deprived areas will provide a rich source of feedback and learning on how LSPs are developing. We will look carefully at the lessons learned from the accreditation process, and draw these out in revised, non-prescriptive guidance to be published next summer. The Government has no intention of imposing a one-size-fits-all approach, or of attempting to micro-manage LSPs through Government guidance or accreditation.

Councils' role on local strategic partnerships

2.35   Councils have a particular responsibility towards LSPs. Our recent guidance reflects this. We look to councils to be the prime movers in instigating LSPs where they do not already exist and in guiding them through their early stages. Once LSPs have been set up the partnerships themselves should decide who leads. As many as one in four LSPs are chaired by partners other than the local authority. This is in keeping with our non-prescriptive approach. That does not mean that once an LSP has been established a local authority's leadership role has ceased. Irrespective of who chairs an LSP, someone needs to take responsibility and be accountable for ensuring that:

- the membership and methods of consultation and engagement are balanced and inclusive;

- difficult decisions are addressed and resolved, not just the easy ones. Those decisions should not simply represent the "lowest common denominator"; and

- the partners properly resource and support the LSP.

2.36 In one sense these responsibilities are shared by all partners. But someone needs to step forward and take a lead on these issues if others are failing to do so. This is a key part of every councils' responsibility as the community leader.

Rationalising partnerships

2.37 Some partnerships are established by statute. Others derive from the requirements of funding or planning activities. Proliferation of these separate partnerships can lead to fragmentation, duplication and inefficiency. LSPs were established, in part, to bring some order to this situation, by placing themselves at the apex of local partnership arrangements and organising existing partnerships on a sensible basis.

2.38 The Government will reduce the number of partnerships it requires. The Regional Co-ordination Unit's review of area-based initiatives will help to reduce the number of partnerships associated with these initiatives. Our proposals to reduce the number of ring-fenced grants and plans will also lead to a reduction in funding and plan-based partnerships.

2.39 Local partners should not have to wait for these deregulatory initiatives to bite. From now on they will have wide discretion as to how and when to rationalise their partnerships. LSPs will be able to slot any statutory partnerships into their emerging structure, for instance as sub-partnerships of the LSP. They will have a free hand to rationalise other partnerships, bringing them together in mergers, nesting them within the LSP and so on. In doing so, partnerships which have a separate legal status will need to maintain a distinct identity. To ensure that these changes are effective, LSPs must develop, discuss and agree them with the partnerships in question.

2.40 Government Offices should be kept informed of any such developments and may be able to provide advice and assistance (but not exercise a veto).

2.41 For the future, the Government will commit itself to working within existing structures wherever possible, signalling to LSPs when we expect a particular policy initiative to be dealt with collectively and looking to LSPs to decide how best to arrange that locally.

Public sector involvement in LSPs

2.42 If LSPs are to succeed, all the relevant public sector partners – as well as those in other sectors – need to play their part. The Government doubts whether a statutory duty will improve the participation of public sector bodies although we will keep this under review. Instead, it will use various other means to encourage engagement with LSPs, including:

- budgetary mechanisms to ensure that public bodies that wish to contribute financially to LSPs have the ability to do so;

- performance management instruments (Public Service Agreements, business plans, service level agreements, management statements and so on);

- line management systems to provide staff with incentives to achieve partnership objectives, and support for staff development and capacity building in relation to partnership working;

- organisational incentives (e.g. through the wider distribution of local PSA rewards); and

- organisational restructuring to provide greater freedom of action to local agencies.

2.43 Levers such as these can have a great effect. In relation to the public bodies accountable to Government, Departments are willing to use any and all of these in order to secure a suitable level of involvement in the work of LSPs as the best way of delivering shared outcomes. During 2002 we will explore in detail with the LGA and other stakeholders how we can best do so, with a view to implementing changes through guidance by April 2003.

Working with business to improve communities

2.44 The Government wants to see councils and businesses in their areas working together to improve local conditions. As part of this, we will legislate to allow Business Improvement Districts (BIDs) to be established in any area where they are backed by the majority of businesses. The BID will be funded by an addition to the business rate. The Government will introduce legislation dealing with such essential issues as the arrangements for the vote on whether to have a BID. Guidance will be provided on how BIDs should work, drawing on existing best practice in establishing and delivering BID-type schemes. We do not wish this to be prescriptive. The Government will encourage the local authority and business organisations to produce this guidance themselves.

PROMOTING EFFECTIVE COMMUNITY ENGAGEMENT AND EMPOWERMENT

2.45 Effective community engagement leads to better decisions and better implementation. Community involvement is a key component of best value, an increasingly important element in the improvements we are making to health services and is an important goal for LSPs in taking forward community strategies and other initiatives. To help build social capital and the capacity of communities to engage in local decisions we have established schemes such as the Community Empowerment Fund, Community Chests and the Community Champions Fund. We shall review the support that Government provides to build community capacity in next year's spending review.

2.46 Councils themselves (both members and officers) need the capacity and skills to engage with and empower their communities. The proposals in Chapter 5 to build the capacity and skills base of officers and members will help here.

2.47 We believe that councils should allow more input from citizens, including giving them better access to council meetings. Area consultation and decision making arrangements have a valuable role to play in helping to involve citizens in decisions which affect them, particularly on neighbourhood issues. We want local authorities to make more use of area forums, public assemblies and citizen's user boards.

2.48 We want people with a stake in the quality of council services to make a more direct contribution to council decision-making. When legislative time is available we will provide greater flexibility for more voting non-councillor members to be co-opted onto overview and scrutiny committees, so that they can take part in activities such as best value reviews.

2.49 We will also develop a programme for promoting civic education and training. Our aim, with local authorities, will be to alert young people to the working of social and public life, their rights and responsibilities, the consequences of the choices they will be called on to make and the means at their disposal for influencing local policies.

2.50 Advisory referendums are a useful way of giving local people a direct say in important decisions affecting their lives. Following through the commitment in our 1998 Local Government White Paper[5] we will legislate at the earliest opportunity to confirm the power of councils to hold referendums on important matters which relate directly to the services they provide and the finances associated with them. Whilst such referendums would be neither obligatory nor binding, they would clearly have considerable status in guiding local decision-making.

GIVING COUNCILS POWERS TO MAKE A REAL DIFFERENCE

2.51 For councils to lead successfully they need the powers to make a real difference to the quality of life of people in their areas. The Local Government Act 2000 provided councils with a new and wide-ranging enabling power to promote the economic, social and environmental well-being of their areas. There is scope to go further. We shall carry through our pledge to provide a wide-ranging power for all councils to charge for discretionary services. And we shall provide new powers for all councils to provide goods and services to other partners, building on our recent proposals[6].

2.52 The quality of our public space has a direct impact on the quality of our lives. That is why we are working on a wide ranging study on improving the public space in preparation for next year's spending review. This includes an examination of the responsibilities, powers, freedoms and enforcement mechanisms currently available to local authorities. In particular, we want councils to have a fully

effective range of powers to deal with social and environmental nuisances. We are already consulting on proposals to enable councils to deal more effectively with abandoned vehicles. We will work with the LGA to extend awareness of current powers and good practice in applying them, and consider changes to the current framework where it is unclear, contradictory or ineffective.

2.53 We will also use deregulatory legislation (such as Regulatory Reform Orders) to simplify existing powers where this would help councils to use them more effectively. For instance, our proposals to replace closely prescribed private sector renewal legislation with a new general power will make it easier for councils to take a strategic approach to housing renewal, giving them more freedom to respond to local priorities.

CONTINUOUS IMPROVEMENT IN THE DELIVERY OF SERVICES

2.54 A council that does not secure real improvements in the services for which it is responsible will not inspire confidence as a community leader. So efforts through best value and the comprehensive performance framework set out in chapter 3 to raise the quality of council services will also help to validate councils' community leadership role.

ALLOWING COUNCILS ROOM TO RESPOND EFFECTIVELY TO LOCAL PRIORITIES

2.55 Chapter 4 sets out a range of proposals on ring-fenced grants and to free councils from other central controls (plans, strategies, consent

---

5 *Modern Local Government: In Touch with the People*, DETR, July 1998, Cm 4014, ISBN 0101401426. http://www.local-regions.dtlr.gov.uk/lgwp/index.htm

6 *Working with Others to Achieve Best Value*, DETR consultation paper, March 2001 http://www.local-regions.dtlr.gov.uk/consult/bestvalue/index.htm

regimes and so on). These will significantly increase councils' freedom to respond to locally-defined needs and priorities.

EXPLOITING NEW TECHNOLOGIES

2.56   New technologies have the potential to transform relations between local people and their councils. They open up possibilities to

- integrate a wide variety of council and other providers' services around the needs of their customers;

- increase participation in council activities such as overview and scrutiny;

- provide more and better information about council and other local services;

- conduct transactions more efficiently and conveniently; and

- improve and speed up access to services and help.

2.57   Exploiting that potential is essential if local government is to keep pace with changing public expectations. Some local authorities are already challenging their 'silos' of service delivery by enabling their citizens to have a single point of access to services in ways which best suit them. There is much scope for extending such initiatives throughout the country. Local authorities were asked to demonstrate their commitment to meeting the Government's electronic service delivery targets by 2005 in their individual Implementing Electronic Government Statements. The task is a significant one and will require sustained commitment over the next few years.

2.58   Many local authorities are using the potential of communications technology to help support community engagement and leadership. To assist this we will redevelop the gateway to internet consultative forums on the UK government portal – *www.ukonline.gov.uk*. We will also commission research on how information and communications technologies can enhance new member and officer roles in councils.

2.59   To help build greater communications capacity, we will work closely with local government on a longer term communications strategy following the outcomes of the current pilot project and the results of our forthcoming research on public participation.

CHAPTER 3
Quality public services

A national framework of standards and accountability and removal of unnecessary burdens and bureaucracy are essential for ensuring that services improve across the board.

Building on the successes and potential of best value and local Public Service Agreements (PSA) the Government will put in place a comprehensive framework for continuous improvement in the quality of local government services to help councils make a real difference for their communities.

Specifically we will:

- clearly define service priorities for local government that have been agreed through the Central Local Partnership (CLP);

- introduce a framework for the overall assessment of performance which addresses these priorities and includes the standards which councils will be expected to deliver;

- publish clear and concise information about councils' overall performance;

- in addition to freedoms for all councils (see chapter 4), grant extra freedoms according to councils' ability to use them to make a real difference, including wide-ranging freedoms for high-performing councils;

- move quickly to a proportionate and co-ordinated inspection regime;

- intervene decisively where councils are failing; and

- publish a national strategy for exploiting the potential of new technologies in local government.

A national framework

3.1   The first of our four principles of public service reform is a national framework of standards and accountability.

3.2   Best value and local PSAs both contribute significantly to improvements in the quality of council services and help councils to serve their communities better. Best value provides the foundation for a much more open and imaginative rethinking of the way services are provided and for councils to work in new and strategic ways with partners from all sectors. Local PSAs, with their focus on voluntary negotiation of stretching targets in return for freedoms and other incentives from Government, promise to accelerate improvements in priority services and are a new way for local and central government to work together. We want to build on the potential of both to realise our shared ambitions for excellence in the quality of services for local communities.

3.3   The Government will put in place a comprehensive and integrated performance framework to help councils deliver better services for their communities. This will include:

- clearly defined priorities and exacting performance standards;

- a framework for performance assessment and proportionate and co-ordinated inspection including regular comprehensive assessments of each council's overall performance;

- extra freedoms and flexibilities for councils which are able to use them to make a real difference for their communities, over and above the universal deregulation described in chapter 4;

- local PSAs to deliver accelerated improvements in priority services supported by additional freedoms; and

- a streamlined and reformed best value framework to help councils manage improvement across all services.

3.4 Information from comprehensive performance assessments combined with clear priorities and standards will lead to:

- targeting of support and inspection resources according to councils' strengths, weaknesses and needs;

- clear and concise public information about councils' performance;

- targeting of additional freedoms to councils with the capacity and track record to make best use of them for their communities;

- easier identification of poor performance and earlier action by councils and others to tackle it;

- better informed negotiations on local PSAs; and

- fewer and more targeted best value reviews.

Priorities for local government

3.5 Local government and those charged with auditing and inspecting councils' performance rightly complain that central government has not been clear enough about what it expects from councils. In future, priorities will be more clearly identified. But this will not be effective if the Government simply specifies targets from above.

3.6 Local government is a partner with central government which, through democratically accountable decision making, identifies and responds to local needs and contributes towards national services through local delivery. Councils will make their most effective contribution if, alongside central government, they take responsibility for key national priorities and instigate corrective action when standards are not being met.

3.7 The Government agrees with the Local Government Association (LGA)[1] that there should be joint ownership of the priorities for local government. Through the Central Local Partnership, we will define a single list of priorities for local government. The list of agreed priorities will inform the national PSA for local government to be developed in next year's spending review.

3.8 The Government's top four public service priorities are education, health, crime and transport (see the box for those to which councils contribute most directly). Councils, often working in partnership with others, have a key role to play in the delivery of each of these. Their education, social care and transport responsibilities are clearly important here, and councils' activities on housing, environmental services, culture, sport, neighbourhood renewal and planning can also contribute. As democratically elected bodies they also have freedom and scope to determine their own priorities locally, based on the needs and aspirations of their communities.

3.9 The Government will expect to see councils' approaches to best value and their local PSAs give clear expression to the priorities in the national PSA as well as locally determined priorities. How priorities are delivered at local level will vary depending on local circumstances. All authorities will be expected to deliver rapid improvements on the priorities identified in the national PSA.

---

[1] *Partnership for Ambition: councils and government working together*, LGA Paper, November 2001.http://www.lga.gov.uk/lga/clp/ambition.htm

Government's priorities for public services

Education

- Transforming secondary education.

- Improving recruitment, retention and quality in the teaching profession.

- Improving access to higher education.

- Raising standards in primary education.

Health

- Improving older people's care and children's services.

- Narrowing the health gap.

Crime

- Reducing crime and the fear of crime.

- Tackling drug abuse.

Transport

- Reducing congestion in large urban areas, increasing bus and light rail patronage, reducing accident rates and contributing to the improvement of local air quality as set out in *Transport 2010: The 10 Year Plan.*[2]

3.10   Local government's commitment to improvement is demonstrated in the LGA's six priority areas for service delivery (see box), some of which reinforce the Government's priorities. The Government has welcomed these and is committed to supporting them. We also welcome the LGA's offer in their recent paper *Partnership for Ambition* of a further commitment to specific actions that support improvements in service delivery, including:

- a specified number of councils to have an Improvement and Development Agency (IDeA) Local Government Improvement Programme visit or re-visit each year;

- poor-performing councils to receive IDeA support;

- a specified number of councils to pilot new ways of joint county-district working; and

- a continuing commitment for a specified number of councils to sign or review their local PSA.

LGA's six priorities for public service delivery

- Supporting children and their families.

- Assisting schools to match the excellence of the best.

- Helping the hardest to reach into work.

- Helping older people live independent lives.

- Delivering higher quality, more reliable bus services.

- Transforming the local environment.

PERFORMANCE MEASURES

3.11   All effective organisations need to know how well they are performing and what their strengths and weaknesses are. The Government must ensure that the priorities on which it was elected are being delivered and that standards are being met across the range of statutory public services.

3.12   Currently there are many overlapping performance measurement frameworks in use by central Government to monitor local government services. The cumulative effect of these can be an overload of confusing measures and a loss of focus on priorities.

3.13   We will move towards a more coherent and integrated system of performance measures

2 *Transport 2010: The 10 Year Plan*, DETR, July 2001, ISBN 1851124136. http://www.dtlr.gov.uk/trans2010/index.htm

across the range of local government services. We will aim in the spending review, in consultation with the LGA, to:

- put in place a national PSA for local government informed by the priorities defined through the CLP, which draws together all the relevant outcome targets;

- devolve these targets to local services through best value and local PSAs;

- ensure that, as far as possible, these local targets are aligned across different public services; and

- update and integrate the Spending Review 2000 floor targets relating to deprived areas.

3.14   In partnership with local government and other stakeholders, we will aim, as part of the coherent and integrated system of performance measures, to put in place a framework in which there are:

- defined standards focused on priority areas identified in the national PSA for local government; and

- clear criteria against which performance can be assessed for each defined standard.

3.15   All authorities will be expected to deliver on these standards. They will be assessed against them through inspections and comprehensive performance assessments. Where councils fail to deliver they will be expected to put things right. Where necessary the Government will take decisive remedial action.

Performance assessment

3.16   High quality council services rely on strong corporate governance from their political and administrative leaders. Where individual services fail the reason often lies in political or administrative shortcomings at the heart of the

organisation. Service-based inspections and assessments do not in themselves provide sufficient means to address overall corporate performance. We will therefore introduce comprehensive performance assessments for all councils building on existing audit, inspections and assessments and including assessments of corporate capabilities.

3.17   These assessments will be a cornerstone of the Government's performance framework for local government. They will provide Government, councils and the public with a clear performance profile for each council. This information will:

- enable a proportionate action plan, linked to the Best Value Performance Plan, to be agreed with each authority to address areas of concern highlighted in the comprehensive performance assessment and to help better target resources for support;

- inform negotiation of targets and freedoms through local PSAs; and

- provide a robust basis for action to tackle poor performance and failure.

3.18   Evidence on councils' performance is currently gathered from a wide range of different assessments. The comprehensive performance assessments will draw these together. Each council's performance and capacity to improve will be assessed, taking into account local circumstances, bringing together:

- performance indicator data (on current performance and past trends);

- OfSTED, the Social Services Inspectorate, the Benefit Fraud Inspectorate and other service based inspections and assessments together with audit reports; and

- a corporate governance assessment of the authority as a whole, undertaken in dialogue with the authority and incorporating an element of peer review.

3.19   The result will be a 'balanced scorecard' compiled by the Audit Commission with assistance from other inspectorates and bodies with an assessment role, and working with councils themselves. This will identify each council as either:

- *high-performing* – near the top of the performance spectrum, with high performance in priority service areas, no poorly performing services and with proven capacity to improve;

- *striving* – not necessarily at the top of the performance spectrum but with proven capacity to improve;

- *coasting* – not at the top of the performance spectrum and with limited or no proven capacity to improve; or

- *poor-performing* – consistently near the bottom of the performance spectrum and with limited or no proven capacity to improve.

3.20   These assessments will be complemented by the new performance rating system for social services described in the box.

3.21   Over time we want all councils to progress up the performance spectrum. Successive comprehensive performance assessments will show which councils are making such progress. They will also show if any councils are standing still or sliding down the performance spectrum.

3.22   In addition, each authority's performance on all the key services will be identified separately using the appropriate inspectorates' assessment wherever these have been satisfactorily completed. The Audit Commission will aim to complete the first comprehensive performance assessments for all upper tier authorities by late 2002 and for district councils by late 2003.

3.23   The Audit Commission is developing, and will pilot, the methodology for the comprehensive performance assessments with other inspectorates and Departments. They will do this in consultation with local government and other parts of the public sector where there

The social services performance rating

Comprehensive performance assessment builds on the development of social services performance ratings, to be published for the first time in Spring 2002-03. The social services performance "stars" will provide judgements of performance for social services in a way that is understandable for the service users and the general public.

Social services performance assessment brings together evidence from indicators, inspections and in-year monitoring. Each year, the Social Services Inspectorate meets with each council to review performance and identify key improvements for the year ahead.

As well as the single star rating for overall social services performance, judgements on services for children and services for adults will be presented. Judgements will be made on the basis of current performance but will also include prospects for improvement.

A range of "freedoms" will be available for the best performers. Three-star councils will have access to their share of the social services performance fund by right, for example. This approach will be extended to other grants and the Government is considering how, for those performing well, planning requirements could be reduced and a lighter touch inspection regime introduced.

The social services performance ratings will feed into the comprehensive performance assessment for all local authority services.

is the potential for joint action, for example with the Commission for Health Improvement.

PUBLIC ACCOUNTABILITY

3.24   To enhance local accountability the Government will publish clear and concise performance information from these assessments for each class of authority. This will include a 'scorecard' available to the public so they can see how well their council is performing. It will also include the overall classifications and a summary of current performance levels for key services.

HIGH-PERFORMING COUNCILS

3.25   Chapter 4 sets out our proposals for deregulation to encourage innovation and creativity, to identify local solutions and to improve performance. In addition, in our manifesto we promised to provide "further flexibility to high-performance authorities, with reformed inspections and more local discretion to encourage civic renewal". This reflects our confidence that the best performing councils will be able to use this additional freedom for the benefit of their areas, and to improve performance still further.

3.26   The additional freedoms that we will provide include:

- a right to have existing ring-fenced grant replaced by targeted grant in any case where the council and Government judge it to be desirable except in respect of grants which have to be passed to schools;

- not being subject to the reserve powers to cap council tax increases;

- more freedom to use income from fines;

- further reductions in plan requirements to be agreed with Government; and

- a reduction in proportion of ring-fencing of Government support for capital investment.

3.27   Chapter 4 sets these additional freedoms in their wider context. As a result of our proposals for new trading powers (see chapter 4), streamlining best value reviews (see below) and a more proportionate and co-ordinated approach to inspections (see below), high-performing councils will also have:

- freedom to trade more widely across the range of their services;

- more discretion over the content and timetable of their best value review programmes; and

- a much lighter touch inspection regime.

3.28   In addition, high-performing councils will have access to further freedoms through their local PSA negotiations.

3.29   Complacency will not be a characteristic of high-performing councils. On the contrary the Government will look to them to lead the way to further service improvements and to share their expertise with other councils. They will also receive targeted support for capacity building and training to help them do this. Subsequent comprehensive performance assessments will look for evidence of this.

3.30   The Government's aim is to see all councils moving into the "high-performing" category by strengthening their capacity to deliver on priority services. This reflects our goal to see widespread excellence across local government. We will keep the package of freedoms for high-performing councils under review. We expect that, over time, further freedoms will be added to the package as they are identified (e.g. through local PSAs) and some of the freedoms in the package could be rolled out more widely if they are shown to be successful in delivering service improvements.

STRIVING COUNCILS

3.31   Further freedoms will be available to striving councils following their comprehensive performance assessment, including through local PSAs.

3.32   We would expect to agree more extensive freedoms for striving councils than for others including access to a package of freedoms approaching that available to high performers. They will also be free to trade in areas where their performance is strong (see chapter 4).

3.33   Striving councils will have a bespoke, lighter touch inspection regime, and more discretion over their best value review programmes. They will receive targeted support for capacity building.

COASTING COUNCILS

3.34   Coasting councils will have their performance monitored against the proportionate action plan they agree following their comprehensive performance assessment (including their best value review programme and audit and inspection programme). They will receive support for capacity building concentrating on areas of weakness. With that support, the Government will expect to see rapid improvement in their overall performance.

3.35   Like others, coasting councils will be able to secure further freedoms through negotiations on their local PSAs where the freedoms can assist in delivering stretching targets to help improve local services. They will also be able to trade in areas where their performance is strong (see chapter 4).

POOR-PERFORMING COUNCILS

3.36   For poor-performing councils it may also be appropriate to temporarily ease some regulatory requirements as part of an overall plan for tackling their weaknesses.

3.37   Poor-performing councils will receive a directed approach to support and capacity building and Government intervention where this is necesssary to tackle corporate or service weaknesses. As described later in this chapter, we will draw from a range of intervention options depending on the nature and seriousness of the weaknesses identified. Their performance will be monitored against the action plan they agree following their comprehensive performance assessment (including their best value review programme).

Proportionate and co-ordinated inspection

3.38   External scrutiny plays a key role in driving up performance. We remain committed to the principle of external inspection and there is a broad consensus amongst all concerned on its potential for delivering improved outcomes.

3.39   The Government recognises that increased inspection activity has led to additional costs for local authorities both directly through fees and indirectly (through the member and staff resources required for inspections). The recent Public Services Productivity Panel review concluded that inspections need to be better co-ordinated and re-focused to reflect and better support council performance.

3.40   We will therefore move quickly to establish a new model of inspection for local government based on the following principles:

- effective co-ordination of inspection across the full range of local authority functions;
- the amount and nature of inspection activity for an authority will reflect its performance profile identified through

the performance assessments and risk analysis, taking account of local priorities; and

- inspection must be an effective component of intervention measures where services are failing.

3.41   In the case of high-performing councils this will lead to a substantial reduction in inspection activity.

3.42   The Government believes that existing institutional arrangements need to be strengthened. In particular:

- the Audit Commission will have a leading role in helping to develop each council's inspection programme working with the other inspectorates. This will flow from the council's action plan following its comprehensive performance assessment;

- we will extend the remit of the Best Value Inspectorate Forum to encompass the full range of local government inspection activity. We will task this new Forum and the Audit Commission with delivering the new inspection regime;

- the Forum will be required to report on progress to a joint Ministerial Group supported by a new unit; and

- in 18 months time the Government will assess progress towards delivering the new inspection regime and consider more fundamental institutional change to drive the process further should this prove necessary.

Tackling poor performance

3.43   The Government will not tolerate poor performance or failing councils and services. They let down the people councils represent and serve. They damage the reputation of the rest of local government. Local government is equally committed to tackling poor performance. Where a council or service is poor or failing we will expect councils to act to put things right and where necessary we will take decisive and tough action.

3.44   Comprehensive performance assessments will provide the basis for a common approach to intervention across Government. Information from those assessments will enable us to identify councils that are failing, on the verge of failing or consistently performing poorly. In discussion with the Audit Commission and other inspectorates, we will establish common criteria across Government which will determine how and when action is taken to tackle failing councils and poor service performance. This will be reflected in a revised intervention protocol with local government. In addition, Ministers will reserve the right to act swiftly to tackle service or corporate failure where a serious risk is identified either to local people or to the well-being of their community. All existing powers for Ministers to intervene where performance is inadequate will be preserved within the new framework.

3.45   Information from comprehensive performance assessments will enable earlier identification of potential corporate failure and poor service performance. Where this occurs we will identify with the authority a package of support provided either from within the local government community or by external bodies. The package will focus on areas of greatest weakness and be designed to remove barriers to greater efficiency and higher quality services. Where support is provided from within the local government community it will generally be under the guidance of the IDeA. If we cannot reach agreement with the authority we will prescribe the measures that are required.

Tackling serious corporate failure

In addition to early intervention through negotiated or imposed peer and external support, the actions described below could be taken where very serious failings are identified.

Transferring functions to other bodies

Where a council is failing, particularly where the authority is in serious financial or corporate difficulty, one option is to require certain functions to be transferred to another body. Options include:

- enforced contracting out of the function to another body such as another local authority, a not-for-profit company or trust or the private sector with the council retaining statutory responsibility for strategic decisions; and

- transferring responsibility in this way but with no residual statutory role for the council.

Administration

Where financial mismanagement is at the root of failure, the law at present requires the council's finance officer to issue a notice suspending all new commitments until the council has met to take decisions. These warning stages are designed to require councillors to rethink their spending decisions. We believe that a stronger process is required where councils are facing persistent financial difficulties with adverse consequences for local people. A further possibility is to appoint an administrator with widely drawn powers to restore solvency while ensuring the continuity of essential services. This would be triggered on public interest grounds and could be the precursor to a longer term negotiated or imposed support package once financial stability has been restored. Administration can also be an effective solution for more general corporate failure.

Franchising management

Incoming managers from a high-performing council or another public body would take on management of the authority under a franchise. Such arrangements could include success-related reward or bonus arrangements. This approach would allow for cross-fertilisation of good practice between authorities, across service boundaries and from other public bodies. It would also promote greater choice of providers for public services.

3.46 Poor-performing and failing councils can expect a comprehensive programme of inspections to monitor progress across the full range of services. We will adopt a more directive approach to best value review programmes and local PSA negotiations, with less discretion for the council about the targets to be met. We will also consider the temporary relaxation of national requirements for less critical services, so that the authority can concentrate on improvements in priority areas.

3.47 Where, following a comprehensive performance assessment, a council is identified as failing with little or no prospect of improvement we will apply early intervention measures. Which measures are used will depend on the specific circumstances of the authority and the nature of the failure. They will include negotiated or imposed peer and external support (described above) and further, tougher actions such as:

- transfer of functions to other providers;

- placing the council into administration; and

- franchising management (where stronger councils are given a role in running weaker ones).

3.48 We will consult on the alternative forms of intervention (including those described in the box) and the way in which they might work in practice. In doing so we will draw on experience of intervention across all services. Tackling poor corporate performance will open new opportunities to change the way in which services are provided and encourage real choice.

Local PSAs

3.49   Local PSAs concentrate on a limited number of important targets for improving performance. Their particular strength is that they are negotiated and agreed between individual councils and Government. Each council makes a commitment in its local PSA to achieving a dozen or so targets for stretching performance focussed on clearly specified outcomes. These targets relate to both the Government's priorities and locally identified priorities. For its part, the Government commits itself to supporting the delivery of national and local priorities by:

- promising performance reward grant for achieving the targets;

- providing a pump-priming grant to help the authority achieve these targets; and

- negotiating freedoms and flexibilities in statutory and administrative requirements that hamper delivery of the targets.

3.50   This year, local PSAs have been agreed with twenty councils in a pilot scheme. All other upper tier authorities have been invited to negotiate agreements over the next two years. Nearly all those authorities have now booked their negotiations and the first four have concluded their agreements. The box gives examples of commitments made by councils and of freedoms agreed by Government in the pilot scheme.

3.51   The Government and the LGA have worked together to develop local PSAs, which have been welcomed by both central and local government. Councils have found them useful in providing a focus for improvements in priority

service areas and have welcomed the opportunity for discussion with senior Government policy officials. Central government has found them useful both as a contribution to meeting national targets and as a forum for developing wide-ranging freedoms to make it easier for councils to deliver high quality services.

3.52   We intend to build on the success of the local PSA pilots to stimulate and reward improvements in performance in those aspects of a council's activities that are of the greatest importance locally and nationally. We will retain the main features of the present scheme described above.

3.53   To ensure greater focus on delivering improvements in priority service areas we will take a more proactive approach to local PSA negotiations. In particular we will:

- approach the council well before negotiations commence to identify a small number of areas in which we will expect their local PSA to include 'stretch' targets. These will focus on those areas within the Government's top four priorities where the council's performance is relatively weak (as identified by the comprehensive performance assessments);

- encourage councils to propose 'stretch' targets in other service areas included in the national PSA for local government, particularly in areas in which their performance is relatively weak; and

- retain a substantial minority of 'stretch' targets for locally identified priorities which matter to local people.

3.54   The Government will continue to assess proposals for freedoms and flexibilities according to their potential to help councils achieve better outcomes. We will recognise stronger performance by agreeing more ambitious freedoms.

Examples of commitments to better outcomes and freedoms and flexibilities agreed in pilot local PSAs

Better outcomes

Education: to increase the percentage of 14 year olds at or above the expected standards for their age in literacy (by 6%), numeracy (by 8%), science (by 7%) and information technology (by 5%). (Previous council target increases without a local PSA were: English 4%; Maths 4%; Science 4%; and IT 3%).

Crime: to reduce the number of domestic burglaries from 4,366 in 1999/2000 to 3,275 in 2003. (Previous council target for 2003 without a local PSA was 3,711.).

Transport: to increase bus use from 31.3m passenger journeys in 1999/2000 to 33.05m in 2003/2004. (Previous council target for 2003/04 without a local PSA was 32.55m.).

Social services: to increase the number of looked after children who are adopted by at least 66% between 1999/2000 and 2003/04. (The expected increase without a local PSA was 33%.)

Waste: to reduce the number of fly tips from 9589 to 8221 between 2000/01 and 2003/04. (The number without a local PSA was expected to rise to 11,986).

Rural areas: to improve access to services in rural areas, reducing poverty and connecting isolated communities, measured by a range of indicators.

Regeneration and neighbourhood renewal: to reduce dependency and increase employment and fulfilment of people in two deprived areas of the county, measured by a range of specific indicators.

Freedoms and flexibilities

- Participation in work on rationalising planning regimes for education and social services.

- Greater ability to transfer funding between education Standards Fund categories.

- Greater certainty of funding from education and crime prevention initiatives.

- Advance piloting of proposals in the Adoption White Paper.

- Return of income from litter fines, to use for street cleanliness projects.

- Agreement with the Driver and Vehicle Licensing Authority to act as agent in removing unlicensed vehicles.

- Permission for provision of joint arrangements in respect of services to address abuse of drugs.

- Experimental lane rental schemes to reduce traffic congestion.

- Better links between local authority closed circuit television monitoring and police radios, overcoming confidentiality problems.

3.55   We will also continue to expect to see evidence in local PSA negotiations that a council is working with other local partners (including other upper-tier councils, single-purpose authorities and district councils) where such collaboration is likely to lead to better outcomes. As local strategic partnerships are developed we will expect them to contribute to the council's shaping of their local PSA and to the delivery of the targets it contains. This will open the way for local PSAs to evolve to cover wider aspects of public services than just those of the local authority. We will retain the flexibility for councils to strike deals with other partners on how to share their pump-priming and reward grants for shared targets, and to request freedoms and flexibilities for their partners to support the delivery of shared targets.

DISTRICT COUNCILS

3.56 District councils are an important feature of the local government landscape especially in rural areas. They deliver important services which affect every household or many households – environmental services, benefits, housing, planning, waste collection, local tax collection, electoral services and so on. This makes districts well placed to benefit from and promote e-technology. They also have an increasingly important role in delivering local environmental improvements (the "liveability" agenda).

3.57 Districts should not work in isolation. The Audit Commission's recent annual best value statement[4] highlights that while some district councils deliver very good services many have limited capacity to improve and innovate. There are particular issues facing small districts which have a limited council tax base and limited capacity to undertake significant discretionary activity, not least because they employ only a small number of officers.

3.58 District councils are best placed to respond and adapt to meet local challenges when working in partnership with others. We continue to believe that collaboration between districts and counties will result in better outcomes than would be achieved by those authorities acting alone, particularly in delivering access to services in rural areas.

3.59 We will continue to provide incentives for county-district co-operation in local PSAs through:

- strong encouragement for county councils' local PSAs to include targets that require working with districts;

- a larger potential reward grant where there is substantial district involvement (reflecting the budgets of participating districts as well as counties); and

- a larger pump-priming grant in recognition of the extra administrative costs of negotiating the involvement of districts.

Streamlining best value reviews and plans

3.60 Best value replaced compulsory competitive tendering, and with it removed the constraints on local authorities which prevented them from working in new and strategic ways with other partners. It is designed to put high standards and the needs of people and communities above cost reduction.

3.61 Best value is already making a difference in delivering service improvements and in closing the gap between the authorities which were lagging well behind the best. Some authorities have shown that step changes in the quality and efficiency of services are possible.

3.62 All this is a promising beginning. Like the Audit Commission, we recognise that there are valuable lessons to be learned from the first year of best value on which we need to act. We also recognise the case for streamlining the best value regime, to enable authorities to use it as an opportunity for radical challenge rather than a bureaucratic process, and to engage citizens and staff in improving services.

3.63 Best value reviews are becoming more strategic and fewer in number. We will introduce further measures to reinforce a more challenging and strategic approach. We will also simplify and reform the best value performance plan.

---

4 *Changing gear: Best Value Annual Statement 2001,* Audit Commission, September 2001, ISBN 1 86240 307 4
http://www.audit-commission.gov.uk/publications/nrchanginggear.shtml

3.64   Our recently published consultation on performance indicators for 2002-03[5] proposed a reduction in the total number of indicators from 123 to 95. This represents a reduction of 23% from 2001-2 and of almost 50% from the high point of 189 indicators in 2000-01. Further reforms will arise from the rationalisation and consolidation of performance measures in next year's spending review.

3.65   These proposals, together with further changes to come following the wider review of best value, will streamline and strengthen the best value framework so that it provides a better basis for developments in:

- performance assessment and inspection;
- local PSAs; and
- intervention where councils or services are failing.

BEST VALUE REVIEWS

3.66   Each council's review programme will be influenced directly by information from the comprehensive performance assessment. In particular:

- high-performing and striving councils will have greater flexibility to determine their review programmes in the light of our intention to remove the requirement to review all of their functions over a five year period; and
- coasting and poor-performing councils will be required to negotiate with the Audit Commission a programme of reviews focusing on particular areas of weakness identified by their

comprehensive performance assessment. For poor-performing councils there will be a greater degree of prescription.

3.67   In each case, review programmes will be negotiated alongside audit and inspection arrangements.

3.68   Challenge remains an essential element of best value reviews. It has often been neglected by local authorities. We will promote a stronger challenge element in best value reviews by:

- encouraging early involvement of auditors and inspectors to ensure that hard questions are tackled at the scoping stage;
- requiring the involvement of 'third parties' (service users, other stakeholders and 'independent' participants) in all reviews, including elements derived from the IDeA's "peer challenge". Chapter 2 describes some measures for strengthening third party involvement in the work of overview and scrutiny committees; and
- issuing clear guidance on the respective roles of executive members and overview and scrutiny committee members in reviews, emphasising the importance of strong corporate leadership within the authority.

3.69   We will also encourage greater use of cross-cutting and joint reviews by:

- building on the findings of councils' comprehensive performance assessments to deliver the priorities set out in the national PSA for local government;
- providing incentives for joint action by tying them more closely to sources of funding such as that for e-government;

---

5 *Best Value Performance Indicators 2002/2003: A Consultation Paper* DTLR, November 2001 http://www.local-regions.dtlr.gov.uk/consult/best02-03/index.htm

- building capacity to manage joint reviews involving third parties; and

- requiring joint reviews as part of a package of remedial measures for poor-performing councils.

BEST VALUE PERFORMANCE PLAN

3.70   The best value performance plan will remain central to our performance framework and provide a focus around which plan rationalisation can take place. It draws together future and past information on councils' performance, plans and finance, and it will feature prominently in the comprehensive performance assessment of each council. Together with the assessment results, it will provide the basis for dialogue with auditors and inspectors on a more integrated and proportionate audit and inspection regime.

3.71   These plans need to be better focused on service delivery priorities, councils' capacity to deliver and financial performance. To achieve this we and councils need to be clearer about the intended audiences for the plan. It is unrealistic to seek to meet the needs of Government, local people and stakeholders, inspectors and auditors in one document.

3.72   The content of the plan will be kept under review to ensure that it is fit for purpose and does not pose excessive burdens. In doing so we will remove the requirement for it to include explicit policy statements on different issues. Instead we will rely on the development of performance indicators such as those on cost-effectiveness. We will move towards a broader annual assessment of the plan and integrate this with traditional audit processes such as the opinion on accounts and the management letter. This judgement will be communicated to stakeholders and the public in the form of a 'report card' on the council's performance and capacity.

3.73   From 2002 we will change the annual date for publication of the full plan to 30 June so that it is based on actual rather than estimated performance information. This will bring it into line with the planned date for publication of councils' annual financial statements. We will require publication of summary information targeted at local taxpayers and service users by 31 March. The summary publication will be integrated with the council tax leaflet sent out with council tax bills from 2002. We are also consulting on medium term proposals for streamlining council tax information[6]. Local authorities will be able to provide this information in a form which helps people to understand it and secures a better fit with other corporate information. The council's monitoring officer and chief executive will be responsibile for ensuring the objectivity and political impartiality of the summary.

BEST VALUE PARISHES

3.74   We will issue separate guidance to best value parishes tailored specifically to their needs. That guidance will include all the streamlining measures described above. When legislation permits, we will pay a grant of £30,000 each year to best value parishes to cover the costs of audit and best value related work such as the preparation of performance plans and the management of reviews.

3.75   Best value should, wherever possible, provide opportunities for principal authorities to delegate functions to parish and town councils and encourage partnership working between the different tiers of local government. We will issue further guidance to principal authorities

---

6 *Improving Communication with Council Tax Payers: A Consultation Paper,* DTLR, September 2001
http://www.local.dtlr.gov.uk/finance/ctax/consult/index.htm

advising them to include in their Best Value Performance Plans their arrangements for working in partnership with parishes on neighbourhood service delivery.

THE REVIEW OF BEST VALUE

3.76 The review of best value will build on these simplifications and reforms and:

- explore ways in which best value can be more focused on higher standards of service;

- ensure best value is neutral as to whether services are provided by the public, private or voluntary sectors, having regard to the need for alternative providers to challenge existing providers and tackle failing services;

- ensure that terms and conditions of staff are fair, both in terms of the work being done and incentives for better performance and, where there is evidence of a two-tier workforce, to propose effective remedies;

- consider how staff can be fully involved in best value; and

- review the scope for providing incentives to managers and employees in the public sector.

DIVERSITY AND CHOICE

3.77 One of our key principles of public service reform is more choice for the consumer including the ability, particularly where quality falls below acceptable standards, to have an alternative provider. We believe that rising expectations amongst the public, together with significant advances in the way in which services can be delivered, make it essential that

there is real variety in the way in which services are delivered, genuine choice of service providers and genuine choice for service users.

3.78 In most cases the highest standards of service provision are more likely to be achieved where there is competition and choice rather than any one supplier dominating the provision of services. We believe it is essential that where services are failing there should be a wide range of alternative options available. Where possible we want to see real choice for the consumer. So we will ensure that the plans drawn up with coasting and poor-performing authorities following their comprehensive performance assessments address the extent to which greater diversity of service provision would improve performance. Where councils do not follow these plans the Government expects the Audit Commission and other inspectorates to recommend the remedial action to be taken by Government.

3.79 Consumer choice comes in various ways. For some services it can come directly so that the public can choose who to go to for a particular service. Where this is possible we want to see it happen: for example in parental choice of school or offering a range of support and care packages for older people. For other services, such as waste collection, choice is less practicable although success in meeting shared objectives, such as on waste recycling, will still depend on meeting householders' preferences. Consumer choice can also come from active participation in council decisions on choice of provider and ultimately through the ballot box.

3.80 No sector – whether public, private or voluntary – is indisputably the right choice in every circumstance. We want to establish the conditions under which all sectors have an opportunity to make a contribution to improving local services, either separately or in partnership. There is no reason why, in principle, these conditions should not apply to all areas of local government responsibility. And we want to give all those delivering high quality and efficient public services, from whichever sector, every incentive to make good use of their experience and expertise to help authorities that are struggling.

3.81   The responsibility for creating the conditions for real choice of this sort rests on all those with an interest in local services. Local authorities, service deliverers, frontline staff and their trades unions all have roles to play. Fair competition and fair employment go hand in hand.

3.82   We will consider urgently the recommendations of the review of best value on ways in which a level playing field can be established for local government services. In the light of the review's recommendations we will consider:

- amending statutory guidance to place greater emphasis on:
  - the use of fair and open competition wherever practicable,
  - diversity in service provision,
  - wider choice of service providers, and
  - analysing, developing and creating markets to encourage diversity, innovation and competitiveness;
- developing better indicators of diversity and choice against which performance can be assessed;
- how best to build capacity so that councils can exploit the opportunities provided by the new powers to trade set out in chapter 4; and
- encouraging better use of best value reviews to identify and tackle delivery options that require partnership with others, including public-public partnerships.

3.83   The Strategic Service Delivery Partnership Task Force has been asked to help evaluate and develop alternative models for service delivery. This development work will make an important contribution to genuine choice for councils and in particular for users of council services.

Exploiting new technologies for better services

3.84   Chapter 2 describes the potential for new technologies to transform the relationship between local people and councils, and to help local government adapt and respond to changing public expectations. New technologies are also critical to improving service quality and cost. These technologies open the way for the public to go to a single website or call centre to find information or transact business. They also reduce information, handling and process costs. These technologies can enable dramatic efficiency gains alongside transformation of the effectiveness of services. They can also open up greater demands on services as access becomes easier.

3.85   This makes it crucial to develop electronic strategies alongside best value reviews and local strategic partnerships. Effective grasp of the transforming potential of e-government will be a key factor in the council's capacity to improve.

3.86   The 100% response rate to the call for councils to prepare Implementing Electronic Government statements is an encouraging sign of local government's readiness to move forward. It is also important for local and national e-strategies to be coherent, so that functional and service plans are thought through from the point of view of local delivery and allow room for local imagination and innovation.

3.87   Early in the new year a national strategy for local e-government will be published. This will provide a platform for central-local co-operation. It will map the building blocks that need to be in place and clarify responsibilities for building national capacity and infrastructure and developing skills and support. It will provide comprehensive information about who is doing what and to what timetable. It will show the way to meeting our target for electronic delivery of all services which can be delivered in this way by 2005. The national strategy will set out an ambitious vision for transformation, integration and change built on exploiting the potential of new technologies to the full.

CHAPTER 4
Freedom to deliver

To realise our common aim of improving people's quality of life councils need greater freedom and wider powers to deliver.

We will:

- provide greater freedom to borrow, invest, trade, charge and set spending priorities;

- abolish Council Tax Benefit Subsidy Limitation;

- cut back on planning requirements, area-based initiatives, consent regimes and other red-tape; and

- take steps to prevent the future imposition of unnecessary new burdens.

Introduction

4.1   The second principle of the Government's programme for public service reform is that effective delivery of national standards requires the devolution of real power and responsibility to local leaders and frontline staff. We have to increase councils' room for action, giving them the powers and freedom they need to innovate and shape services in ways that respond to and meet local needs. We will do this for all councils wherever that will deliver better services. Where councils have the track record and capacity to use substantial extra freedoms for the benefit of their area, we will go further.

4.2   The importance of local government's contribution to improving people's quality of life in areas such as health, education, transport and community safety gives central Government a significant and legitimate interest in the efficiency and effectiveness with which councils deliver services. As a result, Government has sought to influence councils' behaviour, by introducing controls over inputs (e.g. by controlling borrowing, and ring-fencing resources or channelling them through special programmes), processes (by requiring the production of plans or establishment of partnerships) and decisions (e.g. through the introduction of consent regimes).

4.3   There are problems with this approach. Over the years, the cumulative effect has become significant:

- the level of ring-fenced grant is in danger of rising to levels that seriously restrict councils' financial room for manoeuvre;

- councils are now required to produce some 66 separate plans and strategies, with top tier councils alone required to produce more than 40;

- the Regional Co-ordination Unit has identified some 30 key initiatives targeted at deprived areas and neighbourhoods.

4.4   This accumulation of central requirements and initiatives can become counter-productive, especially if – as has often been the case – measures are not focused on the clear delivery of outputs and outcomes, and are introduced without considering their potential to increase bureaucracy and inefficiency.

4.5   That is not to say that these mechanisms are of no value. They can be an effective and appropriate response in certain circumstances, notably to kick start action on a national priority that is not yet being effectively addressed at local level. But Government needs to use them in a more measured and considered way. Too often they are seen as a first resort, rather than as one of a range of policy responses. Once introduced, Government is often slow to remove or wind them up, even when they have served their purpose. Too little account is taken of the cumulative effect that such measures can have – including the attendant dangers of fragmentation, duplication and rigidity in the efforts of councils and their partners to tackle local problems.

4.6   The new arrangements described in chapter 3 will allow Government to shift its focus to the assured delivery of outcomes through a national framework of standards and accountability, and away from controls over inputs, processes and local decisions. In chapter 6 of part II of this publication we set out proposals to promote sound financial management and responsibility. With these initiatives in place, many of the existing controls over processes and finances will become unnecessary. So over the course of this Parliament we will give councils more space to innovate, to respond in ways that are appropriate to local circumstances, and to provide more effective leadership.

4.7   We will provide greater freedom for councils to borrow, invest, trade, charge and set spending priorities. We will reduce the number of plans councils are required to produce at Government's behest, rationalise area-based initiatives, abolish a large number of consent regimes, and tackle a number of other items of regulation or red tape. And we will put in place effective mechanisms to prevent the imposition of new and unnecessary burdens.

Freedom to borrow and invest

4.8   We will abolish the existing system of credit approvals. It will be replaced by a local prudential regime under which individual authorities will be responsible for deciding how much they can afford to borrow, in accordance with the code which CIPFA is developing. There will be reserve powers to set a national borrowing limit in circumstances where the total local authority borrowing seems likely to result in a level of expenditure which the economy could not afford. There will also be reserve powers to re-impose Government control on authorities which abuse the new freedom. Instead of controlling the borrowings of all councils, the Government will intervene only where an authority proves unable to discharge the responsibility itself.

4.9   The amount of borrowing that an authority can afford will normally depend on the revenue income available to service debt after meeting other spending commitments. It would not be prudent for authorities to borrow against the security of their capital assets and we shall retain the present prohibition on the mortgaging of local authority property.

4.10   This new approach to capital investment will also cover housing, giving authorities freedom to borrow to the extent that they can afford to service the additional debt from their existing resources. We believe that housing finance must remain separate from other funding. It would be wrong for council housing either to subsidise or be subsidised by the general council taxpayer. But we will simplify housing finance and eliminate unnecessary divergence between housing and the rest of the finance system.

4.11   When the new prudential regime comes in, we will end the unnecessarily complex 'receipts taken into account' mechanism, and not replace it with an alternative system[1]. This will mean that authorities will no longer have part of their capital receipts taken into account in the allocation of Government capital support. The current housing 'set aside' arrangement will be replaced by a simpler housing capital receipts pooling system that will apply to all housing receipts, including those received by debt free authorities.

[1] See paragraph 4.32 of part II.

4.12   We will create new options to allow authorities to get best value when they invest the funds they hold. We are consulting on giving authorities access to commercial 'money market funds' and to a similar public sector fund operated by the Public Works Loan Board. We propose to make the latter available in advance of the new legislation.

Greater freedom to trade and charge

4.13   The Government wants to see a dynamic and entrepreneurial public sector which will increase diversity and choice in the delivery of public services. In March, we published a consultation paper with proposals to allow best value authorities to supply and charge for goods and services to others in the public, private and voluntary sectors.[2] The proposals were intended largely to replace reliance on the Local Authorities (Goods and Services) Act 1970, which restricts local authorities' trading powers to dealings with other authorities and designated public bodies.

4.14   We will go further than the proposals in the consultation paper and provide wider powers to trade for all authorities, where this helps achieve best value in the delivery of public services. Councils should be able to trade in any service in which they have a strong performance on delivery. High performers will therefore be able to trade across a wide range of their services. Trading will not be subject to any centrally imposed financial limit or be limited to the exploitation of existing assets. We will provide incentives to good service providers to take on new work and build their capacity to provide services to others. We will publish statutory

guidance on the use of these powers, which will provide the necessary safeguards for taxpayers, local service users and businesses. This guidance will ensure that councils do not distort markets through cross-subsidation and other forms of unfair competition. It will also be tailored to the effectiveness of each council, giving the best performers the widest freedom and flexibility to use the new powers.

4.15   In addition, we will give authorities the power to charge an appropriate fee for providing discretionary services.

Greater freedom to set spending priorities

4.16   We have undertaken a review of ring-fenced grant. We conclude that ring-fencing remains an important means of bringing about change, for example ensuring that councils and schools devote sufficient attention to areas that have been neglected in the past. However, the growth in ring-fencing is excessive – from 5% of all grant in 1997 to 12% this year and on present trends to 15% in 2003-04. This growth threatens to erode local decision-making responsibility, limit authorities' ability to tackle important local environmental priorities (such as litter, graffiti and public spaces) and to increase council tax levels.

4.17   We will therefore restrict ring-fencing to cases which are genuine high priorities for Government, and where we cannot achieve our policy goal by specifying output or outcome targets. Any new ring-fenced grant schemes will be time-limited and have no match-funding requirements, other than for very small pilot schemes. All authorities will benefit from these reforms, which demonstrate that the

---

2 *Working with Others to Achieve Best Value*, DETR consultation paper, March 2001 http://www.local-regions.dtlr.gov.uk/consult/bestvalue/index.htm

Government is committed to reducing the level of ring-fenced funding. High-performing councils will have a right to have existing ring-fenced grant replaced by targeted grant in any case where they and Government judge it to be desirable except in respect of grants which have to be passed to schools. We will also restrict the proportions of ring-fenced capital support.

4.18   We have already announced that we will allow local authorities to use the money from fines for dog fouling and littering to provide additional spending to enhance the local environment. We also intend to make surplus revenue from parking fines available for additional spending on local environmental improvement rather than just transport projects. We will give high-performing authorities complete freedom to decide how to spend the income from dog fouling, littering and parking fines. In addition, we will review other new and existing powers to levy civil penalties with a presumption that further freedoms can be offered to high-performing authorities. The powers under which councils levy fines are contained in various legislation. Suitable amendments to these will be made in order to provide the flexibilities we propose.

Other finance freedoms

4.19   We will abolish council tax benefit subsidy limitation. We are consulting on giving councils greater freedom to decide council tax discounts and exemptions. We will also not use the reserve power to cap high-performing authorities.

4.20   Details of our plans to modernise capital funding arrangements are set out in chapter 6 and in part II of this publication.

Cutting back on plan and strategy requirements

4.21   A recent study by the Department of Transport, Local Government and the Regions (DTLR) has identified some 66 plans which councils are required to produce at Government's behest. Three Departments – DTLR, the Department of Health and the Department for Education and Skills (DfES) – are responsible for 48 of these.

4.22   The Government wants to see sustainable development become a mainstream issue for local authorities, their partners, and local communities. We believe that the most effective way to achieve this is to subsume Local Agenda 21 strategies within statutory community strategies (which are required, by law, to promote sustainable development[3]). Many councils have already done this, and we encourage others to follow suit.

4.23   Our guidance on local strategic partnerships (LSPs) published in March[4] recognised the link between community strategies and neighbourhood renewal strategies. Both strategies will be prepared by LSPs, and there are clearly important links between efforts to renew the most deprived neighbourhoods and wider initiatives to improve quality of life in an area. LSPs will therefore be free to decide whether to combine these strategies in a single document. If they decide to do this, the specific measures for tackling neighbourhood renewal should not be lost in doing so.

4.24   The requirements to produce corporate capital strategies and asset management plans (AMPs) are relatively new. They were introduced as part of the efforts within the single

---

3   Section 4 of the *Local Government Act 2000*

4   *Local Strategic Partnerships: Government Guidance*, DETR, March 2001, Product code: 01LG9011. http://www.local-regions.dtlr.gov.uk/lsp/guidance/index.htm

capital pot to improve the way in which authorities develop their capital investment strategies and promote better use and management of assets. Corporate capital strategies and AMPs will be needed for councils' own purposes. As soon as councils are producing corporate plans to a sufficiently robust standard, the requirement for these plans to be submitted to Government will be dropped.

4.25   Education AMPs were developed and introduced in advance of the corporate AMPs and serve significantly wider purposes. They inform directly allocations of capital support to councils as well as providing a basis for local improvement through the benchmarking of data and performance. They are still in the process of development, for instance to support better management of capacity and more robust options appraisal. These and other differences mean that the requirement to submit Education AMPs, including information on priorities and processes will continue. DfES will look to reduce the information needed for high performing councils, and will publish guidance on improving the joining up of Education AMPs with councils' wider, corporate document.

4.26   The recent Housing Investment Programme (HIP) Review has already removed the requirement on local authorities to make a separate HIP submission. HIP performance assessments are now based on annual Housing Business Plans and Strategies which councils need to prepare in order to discharge their responsibilities. Legislation currently before Parliament introduces homelessness strategies. The DTLR will publish guidance to bring these plans together under the umbrella of the housing strategy. The intention is to move to a single strategy that is current for 3-5 years once the documents have reached a 'fit for purpose' standard.

4.27   The green paper on development planning proposes a radical restructuring of and reduction in the number of development plans.

4.28   The Department of Health has recently carried out a major review of the plans it requires in relation to social services. The review concluded that there is scope for a significant reduction in the numbers of plans. Ministers have accepted those conclusions. As a result, a significant proportion of the Department's plans will be abolished, merged, or otherwise streamlined.

4.29   DfES guidance on the new Accessibility Strategies[5] will allow these to be subsumed within an existing plan of Local Education Authorities' choice. The rolling together of a number of other plans into a single Local Education Strategy, currently being piloted by five councils through local Public Service Agreements (PSAs), will be extended to other authorities if the pilots are shown to be successful. And the DfES will look favourably at further suggestions for plan rationalisation which come forward in local PSA negotiations.

4.30   We will no longer require the production of a separate Air Quality Management Action Plan where an air quality problem arises because of transport pollution. Instead, councils will be free to address this through their Local Transport Plan. And the Department of the Environment, Food and Rural Affairs will remove the requirement to produce the Waste Recycling Plan once the statutory requirement to produce a Municipal Waste Management Strategy is in place.

4.31   With the introduction of the new performance management framework, the Department for Culture, Media and Sport will review the amount of information required of councils in the Annual Library Plan with a view to streamlining those requirements and the

---

[5] Introduced by sections 28D and 28E of the Disability Discrimination Act 1995 and amended by the Special Educational Needs and Disability Act 2001.

process. This will be done in conjunction with expert library bodies.

4.32   The White Paper on Police Reform[6] sets out proposals for Crime and Disorder Reduction Partnerships and Drug Action Teams to work together in developing and implementing local crime and disorder reduction strategies and the drugs strategies. Proposed mergers of these two groups will help improve efficiency and delivery.

Streamlining the requirements that remain

4.33   The remaining requirements should work, as far as possible, with the grain of councils' own activities. We will work with the Local Government Association (LGA) to review the remaining plans in order to:

- identify further scope for rationalisation with the aim of a reduction of at least 50% from current levels; and

- identify the minimum requirements which Government needs councils to fulfil and seek to amend those requirements that remain so they fit as effectively as possible with councils own planning requirements.

4.34   This review will be informed by the work undertaken by the Children and Young Peoples Unit on rationalising planning for childrens' and young people's services[7], and the inter-departmental component of the Department of Health's review of health and social care plans. Our review of emergency planning will look at the scope for rationalising the Civil Defence Plan, Pipeline Safety Plan and the Control of Major Accident Hazards Plan.

4.35   For high performing authorities there will be opportunities to negotiate and agree additional freedoms from requirements to produce plans.

Rationalising area-based initiatives

4.36   Local joined-up action designed to tackle specific area-based challenges has an important role to play in improving services for local people. However, there is a need to rationalise and streamline these area-based initiatives (ABIs), in order to maximise local flexibility and minimise bureaucracy.

4.37   Government is currently reviewing ABIs with a view to amalgamation, integration or mainstreaming. Government Offices for the Regions and local government are engaged in this process. We have already announced steps to bring Education Action Zones together with the Excellence in Cities programmes. An action plan to rationalise the Government's small grants programme for community groups will be published in shortly.

4.38   The Government will extend opportunities for the pooling of ABI budgets at local level to deliver initiatives more effectively. A pilot study currently taking place in one council is considering the pooling of budgets for a range of initiatives including the Single Regeneration Budget, Education Action Zones, the Neighbourhood Renewal Fund and the Children's Fund.

---

6   *Policing a new century: a blueprint for reform*, Home Office, December 2001, Cm 5326, ISBN: 0-10-153262-8, www.policereform.gov.uk

7   The Government's new Strategy for Children and Young People was published for consultation in November. *Building a Strategy for Children and Young People* includes proposals for simplified and rationalised planning arrangements for children and young people's services, in line with the proposals in this white paper. To obtain a copy of the strategy, visit the website at www.cypu.gov.uk or call the Unit's dedicated phone line on 020 7273 1120.

4.39   The Government has also encouraged local government both directly and through their membership of LSPs to play a key role in the rationalisation and streamlining of ABIs. We are also considering how LSPs can be given greater discretion to widen targeted programmes to meet local circumstances.

Abolishing consent regimes

4.40   Requirements on local authorities to seek Government consent before taking action weaken local accountability and stifle innovation. With the introduction of the Regulatory Reform Act 2000 Government now has the means to repeal unnecessary consent regimes without resort to primary legislation. Decisions have already been taken to repeal 52 consent regime powers. Decisions on a further 30 powers outstanding from the 1997 Efficiency Scrutiny's recommendations will be taken shortly.

Removing other "red tape"

4.41   In a joint exercise with the LGA the Cabinet Office Regulatory Impact Unit has identified some 61 items of potential red-tape that would benefit from closer examination with a view to their removal. Several of these are dealt with by the proposals elsewhere in this white paper, in the Planning Green Paper, or in the current review of road traffic legislation. On the others, the Government will work jointly with the LGA to review each item, and take the necessary steps to remove unwarranted burdens. We will publish the joint study report with the LGA and Cabinet Office early next year. This report will contain
a timetable for completing and implementing the review.

Controlling new red tape

4.42   Government's efforts to reduce red tape will be of little benefit to local government unless effective means are in place to minimise the imposition of new requirements. The measures described above will be accompanied by the piloting of a new policy evaluation tool – the *Policy Effects Framework* – which will seek to prevent the imposition of unnecessary burdens. We need to ensure that we establish a consistent gateway process on the introduction of new plans, performance indicators, ring-fenced grants and other regulatory controls.

4.43   As noted earlier, planning requirements can serve a useful purpose in certain circumstances. But the need to introduce a further plan needs to be considered alongside alternative ways of achieving the policy goal in question. Where the conclusion is that a new plan is needed, we will:

- consider how the proposed requirement fits in with council processes as well as Government's needs; and

- seek to agree any new requirement with local government, rather than simply imposing it.

4.44   Ring-fenced grants can also have a useful role to play in certain circumstances, particularly to kick-start action on a priority area which is not being addressed. Before introducing any new ring-fenced grant we will have regard to the criteria described in paragraph 4.17 above.

CHAPTER 5
Support for councils

Support for capacity building for councils and training for members and officers is an important part of our proposals to see excellent local government services and leadership.

We will:

- conduct a wide-ranging review of support for capacity building and training to develop proposals for more effective use of resources;

- develop and pilot a gateway review process to support complex, high risk or novel procurement projects; and

- develop the Beacon Councils Scheme, integrate it with our performance framework and maintain its focus on peer support and best practice guidance for frontline service delivery.

Building capacity and supporting councils

5.1   The ambitious agenda for local government set out in this white paper presents significant challenges to local authorities, their members and staff. They need to access a range of new skills and build their management capacity to meet these challenges and to take full advantage of the greater freedom, new powers and increased responsibility we are proposing. The Government is determined to ensure that councils, members and officers all have the support they need to build their capacity to deliver strong and confident community leadership and high quality public services. In particular there is a need to build up capacity and skills in:

- strategic leadership;

- effective overview and scrutiny; and

- partnership working, performance management, project management, new technologies and commissioning and procurement.

5.2   The Improvement and Development Agency (IDeA), Employers' Organisation, Public Private Partnership Programme (4Ps), Social Care Institute for Excellence, Strategic Partnering Taskforce and our Local Government Modernisation Team all make significant and valuable contributions. Their work will continue to evolve to meet new needs. But more needs to be done.

5.3   In the context of next year's spending review we will undertake a wide-ranging review of support for councils and training for councillors and council staff. Our proposals for more effective and co-ordinated support will focus on:

- rationalisation of the current wide range of funding streams available to councils;

- more effective targeting to address each council's strengths, weaknesses and needs as revealed by the comprehensive performance assessments;

- making the best use of scarce skills; and

- facilitating effective exchange of skills and ideas between local authorities and between local authorities, central government and other public, private and voluntary sector organisations.

5.4   This chapter describes some actions we will be taking now and some of the options we will be considering during the spending review. We would welcome views on the issues and proposals put forward in this chapter[1].

---

[1] Responses should be sent by 28 February 2002 to Ben Turner, DTLR, 5/B6 Eland House, Bressenden Place, London, SW1E 5DU, e-mail Ben.Turner@dtlr.gsi.gov.uk. In line with normal practice, Ministers may wish to publish responses and make them available to Parliament. Should respondents wish their comments to be treated in confidence they should make this clear in their response. All responses may nevertheless be included in statistical summaries of the comments received and views expressed.

Resources and delivery

5.5   The Government will consider the effectiveness of current support and funding. All Government Departments will examine, with the Local Government Association (LGA) and others, the roles, capabilities and potential of the bodies currently providing support for capacity building in local government, and consider:

- whether a different institutional structure is needed, and if so if there is a need for a new joint central-local body to plug gaps and remove overlaps in provision and co-ordinate support more effectively;

- how existing funds can be consolidated and rationalised to provide more effective and co-ordinated support to councils, including the option of a single fund;

- how funding should be distributed and targeted, including the possibility of a new targeted grant to provide councils with resources to build capacity; and

- whether the current balance between revenue and capital support for capacity building and training is right.

Training and development

5.6   Better targeted and co-ordinated resources will improve the effectiveness of investment in training and development for members and officers. The steps which councils and Government can take to improve the quality of member and officer training include:

- joint member and officer training;

- capacity building for senior management teams as well as individuals;

- self-managed learning supported by experienced mentors;

- joint training across sectors;

- joint training for central and local government officials, and across the public sector;

- wider use of secondments and job shadowing between central and local government and between local government and other public, private and voluntary sector organisations;

- a 'directory' for member and officer training; and

- effective use of new technologies such as e-briefings, e-learning and telephone and video conferencing.

5.7   The Government will look at how support can best be provided for these activities and what more the Government can do to facilitate and encourage them.

Making the best use of scarce skills

5.8   For the scarcest skills it may not be cost-effective or realistic to build up sufficient in-house resources for all councils to be self-reliant. For example, local authorities may only be involved in one 'big ticket' procurement every few years and may need to import the necessary expertise. This was recognised by the Taskforce led by Sir Ian Byatt and reflected in their report on procurement in local government[2].

5.9   The Government agrees with the Taskforce that the use of gateway review processes by local authorities will help improve the quality of delivery for complex, high-risk or

---

[2] *Delivering Better Services for Citizens – A review of local government procurement in England*, DTLR, August 2001, ISBN 1851124853 http://www.local-regions.dtlr.gov.uk/consult/betterservices/report/index.htm

novel procurement in local government. We will support the implementation of this approach as part of the wider initiatives on capacity building. We will do so in co-ordination, as appropriate, with the Office of Government Commerce, Partnerships UK, the 4Ps and the IDeA. We will work with these agencies on a number of other initiatives to help improve local government procurement, including:

- brokerage (helping local authorities and other public bodies come together to work in partnership and to gather market intelligence);

- mentoring;

- training;

- an advisory service;

- good practice guidance; and

- standard core contract documentation.

5.10 We will also work with the private and voluntary sectors to maximise their contribution to building capacity and diversity.

Peer support and best practice

5.11   The dissemination and sharing of best practice has an important part to play in developing and improving councils' capacity and capability to deliver quality local services and leadership. There is a great deal of good practice within local government and we need to maximise the opportunities for councils to learn from one another.

5.12   The Government recognises and welcomes the significant contributions made by the IDeA's Local Government Improvement Programme

and other initiatives such as IDeA *Knowledge* and *Learning*. We need to build on these.

5.13   The Government will encourage district councils to make more use of the Local Government Improvement Programme, particularly in the run up to their comprehensive performance assessments. District councils will be able to focus their resources for capacity building on weaknesses identified in their peer review report.

5.14   Our review of support will also look at proposals to:

- include in all pathfinder and similar schemes an explicit requirement, as a condition of award, that councils work with one or more authorities whose performance is weak in the service in question;

- encourage high-performing authorities to work with poor-performing councils, perhaps by twinning high-performing authorities with poor-performing authorities; and

- establish a pool of accredited members and senior officers who will be available to support and advise other authorities.

BEACON COUNCILS

5.15   Independent research has identified the considerable progress achieved by the Beacon Councils Scheme and its contribution to improving services[3]. Attaining Beacon status provides national recognition for front-line staff delivering public services and helps all councils to learn and to improve their own performance. The research and feedback from councils and the Beacon Councils' Advisory Panel have identified a need to clarify the future of the

---

[3] *Leading and Learning: perceptions and attitudes toward the Beacon Council Scheme and motivations for attending events* (Rashman, L. Hartley, J. and Gulati, A., August 2000) and *Monitoring and Evaluation of the Beacon Council Scheme: report of the process outcomes evaluation* (Hartley, J. Rashman, L. Downe, J. and Storbeck, J., to be published shortly)

scheme, examine the resources available to it and streamline the application process. We will retain the scheme, including the principle of voluntary participation, and we will:

- integrate it with the comprehensive performance assessments set out in chapter 3, for example by using those assessments to inform the Panel's consideration of applications for beacon status;

- provide greater certainty about the future of the programme and strengthen links with best value reviews by moving to a longer-term rolling programme of Beacon themes;

- open up the scheme to applications from all best value authorities, including national parks authorities, police authorities and best value parish and town councils;

- develop with the IDeA a more effective approach to disseminating best practice; and

- consider the adequacy and effectiveness of the financial support for Beacon Councils, as part of our wider review of support.

Recruitment and retention

5.16   Terms and conditions of local government employment are rightly a matter for local authorities themselves to determine. We are aware of concerns from councils that recruitment and retention of some high calibre staff is becoming increasingly difficult. So we will work with the LGA and the Employers' Organisation on a strategy to help local government recruit and retain the right staff. In doing so we will examine:

- the option of a 'Graduate Management Programme' for local government, similar to the Civil Service Fast Stream;

- the feasibility of central recruiting in relation to specialist skills, to build up a cadre of specialists that could be trained and deployed flexibly, possibly through regional centres of excellence; and

- how councils can be encouraged to provide incentives to front-line staff to deliver performance improvements, including more imaginative pay frameworks.

Working with others

5.17   An important method of increasing capacity is through working with others, whether that is other local authorities, the wider public sector or the voluntary and private sectors. This encourages cross-fertilisation of ideas and skills and provides access to the resources, technology and scarce skills that many councils urgently need.

5.18   Through initiatives such as the Strategic Partnering Taskforce we will ensure that advice is available to authorities on new ways of working and new models of service delivery. This will include encouraging authorities to provide services to others using the new trading powers described in chapter 4.

5.19   If there is to be genuine support for the principle of working with others to deliver high quality services, then employees and their trades unions need to be confident that improvements do not come at the expense of their terms and conditions. The Government recognises that high quality services depend on highly motivated staff and employers who recognise their staff as a valuable resource. The review of best value (see chapter 3) will make recommendations on how this can be achieved as part of the best value process. Both trades unions and employers share a common interest in making sure that best value achieves high standards of service.

CHAPTER 6
Investing for improvement

A sound local government finance system needs to promote local financial freedom and responsibility, address and minimise unfairnesses and be readily understood by those it serves.

We will implement freedoms proposed in last year's green paper *Modernising Local Government Finance* and we will go further by:

- introducing a number of additional reforms which give all local authorities greater

control over how they raise, spend and invest their money, and which reduce bureaucracy; and

- giving extra freedoms to high-performing and striving authorities.

Alongside these new freedoms, we will introduce measures to promote good financial management at the local level.

We will ensure that changes to the local government finance system are managed sensibly.

Where we start from

6.1   The local government finance system should help authorities deliver on national and local priorities. It should also reinforce local decision making.

6.2   The local government finance system which we inherited in 1997 did not meet these criteria. In particular:

- Government grant was declining in real terms. Services were suffering. There was serious neglect of capital investment and maintenance;

- public expenditure totals and grant formulae were revised annually. There was no certainty about future funding. So, authorities could not plan ahead;

- too much power was vested in Whitehall. Local authorities had little control over their own income. They required Government permission to borrow;

- the distribution of Government grant was unfair. Resource was not always allocated where it was most needed and would do most good; and

- the system was too complicated. Councillors could not understand how

grants were allocated. Head-teachers could not understand how their budgets were set. Council taxpayers could not understand their bills.

6.3   In the last Parliament, we concentrated on tackling the first two problems. We have provided substantial real increases in revenue grant and support for capital investment (see charts). We have delivered greater predictability and stability – by setting three-year expenditure totals in the spending reviews, by freezing the standard spending assessment (SSA) formulae, by introducing floors and ceilings on the grant increases for individual authorities, and by making earlier announcements on ring-fenced grants and credit approvals. Local authorities are better funded than they were, and can plan ahead with greater confidence.

6.4   It is now time to tackle the outstanding issues. We need to:

- promote local freedom and responsibility, and strip out unnecessary bureaucracy;

- address the unfairnesses in revenue grant distribution; and

- try to make the finance system more intelligible to those it serves.

Central government support for local authority revenue expenditure

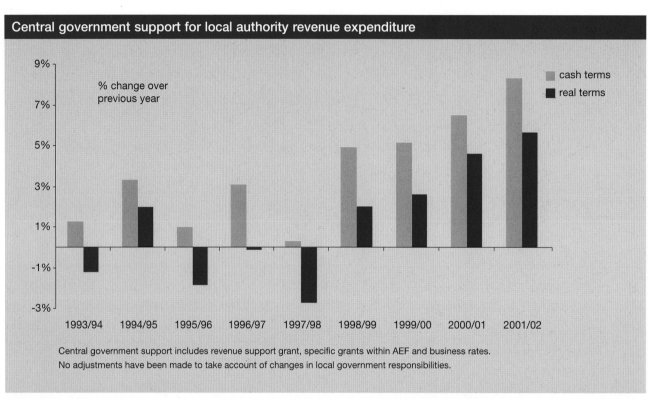

% change over previous year

- cash terms
- real terms

1993/94 1994/95 1995/96 1996/97 1997/98 1998/99 1999/00 2000/01 2001/02

Central government support includes revenue support grant, specific grants within AEF and business rates.
No adjustments have been made to take account of changes in local government responsibilities.

Central government support for local authority capital expenditure

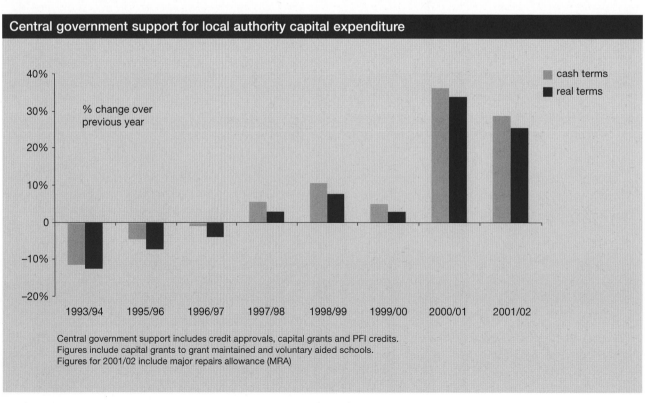

% change over previous year

- cash terms
- real terms

1993/94 1995/96 1996/97 1997/98 1998/99 1999/00 2000/01 2001/02

Central government support includes credit approvals, capital grants and PFI credits.
Figures include capital grants to grant maintained and voluntary aided schools.
Figures for 2001/02 include major repairs allowance (MRA)

6.5   Chapter 4 sets out our proposals for substantial freedoms and flexibilities for all councils and additional freedoms for councils depending on their performance. It includes proposals for greater financial freedom and responsibility such as:

- abolishing council tax benefit subsidy limitation for all authorities;
- greater freedom for all authorities to decide council tax discounts and exemptions;
- the power for all authorities to charge an appropriate fee for providing discretionary services;
- more freedom for all authorities on borrowing and investments;
- the right for high-performing councils to have ring-fenced grant replaced by targeted grant in any case where they and Government judge it to be desirable except in respect of grants which have to be passed to schools;
- not using the reserve power to cap the council tax increases of high-performing councils; and
- greater freedom for high-performing councils to decide how to spend the income from certain civil penalties.

6.6   The remainder of this section summarises the other key elements of our local government finance reforms all of which are set out in detail in part II of this publication.

Local authorities' income

6.7   Local authorities raise about one quarter of their income from council tax and about 11% from fees and charges. Most of the remaining two-thirds of their income comes from Government grants, which are funded from national taxes including the business rate. It is often argued that this balance between national and local taxes has an adverse impact on local authorities' autonomy, but there is little hard evidence for or against this view, and there is no consensus on how the balance might be shifted. Once we have done some further analysis of this, we shall establish a high-level working group, involving Ministers and senior figures from local government, to look at all aspects of the question – reviewing the evidence and looking at reform options.

6.8   We do not consider there are any quick or easy ways of securing a major shift in the balance of funding, particularly given the need to respect the views of taxpayers and to ensure that financial reform does not become a distraction from the delivery agenda. However, we need to be clear what the longer-term reform options are. We also need to consider whether there are more modest reform options that could be pursued more quickly.

6.9   As part of our deregulatory agenda, we are abolishing council tax benefit subsidy limitation, and we will not use the reserve capping powers against high-performing authorities. We are consulting on giving councils greater freedom to decide council tax discounts and exemptions. And we will make council tax bills more transparent, so that taxpayers can see by how much different authorities are increasing their council tax.

6.10   We will also bring the council tax up-to-date. Bills based on new property values will issue in 2007. We will legislate to require ten-yearly revaluations in the future. A revaluation should have no impact on the total amount of council tax raised. Ahead of revaluation, we will listen to the views of taxpayers and local government about council tax bands and related matters. We shall introduce legislation to make it clear that additional council tax valuation bands can be created without new primary legislation.

Financial support from Government

6.11 Government support for revenue spending takes the form of ring-fenced grant (which has restrictions on how it is spent) or general grant (which has no such restrictions). As described in chapter 4 any new ring-fenced grants will be time-limited and have no match-funding requirements other than for very small pilot schemes. We will also give high performing councils the right to have ring-fenced grant replaced by targeted grant in any case where they and the Government judge it to be desirable except in respect of grants which have to be passed to schools.

6.12 Most general grant will be allocated by new formulae. We will not base grant decisions on the Government's assessment of authorities' own forward spending plans.

6.13 We will introduce new grant formulae for 2003-04 which will replace SSAs. We aim to make the new formulae more intelligible than existing SSA. We want to move away from the use of regression analysis which replicates past patterns of spend and to focus on up-to-date evidence on why the cost of providing services varies. We will take more account of the fixed costs that authorities face. Floors and ceilings will set limits on the annual change in grant. They will ensure that all authorities receive a reasonable increase in grant.

6.14 Once the new formulae are in place, there will be a further 'freeze' on formula changes for 2004-05 and 2005-06, except where there are changes in the functions of councils, or the financing of particular services. We will work with local government with the aim of introducing a safety-valve grant in 2004-05. The grant will be available to authorities which have high levels of council tax and low unit costs, but which do not benefit from the new grant formulae.

6.15 We will consult local government about the best way of providing Government support for capital investment under the new regime. We will also:

- reform the single capital pot, to reduce the amount of ring-fencing of capital support available to high performing and striving authorities;

- abolish the unnecessarily complex 'receipts taken into account' mechanism when the prudential borrowing system comes in (the current housing 'set aside' arrangement will be replaced by a simpler housing capital receipts pooling system that will apply to all housing receipts, including those received by debt free authorities); and

- phase out the requirement for local authorities to send their corporate capital strategies and asset management plans to Government. Requirements for service specific AMPs, such as that for Education, although reduced for high performing authorities, will continue in order to fulfil their specific purposes such as enabling needs related resource allocation.

6.16 We will maintain the Bellwin scheme of support for authorities faced with floods or other emergencies. We will reform the scheme along the lines recommended by the joint DTLR/local government review group, by setting its funding on a sounder footing and issuing clearer guidance on what costs are eligible for support.

Parish and town councils

6.17 We will make the financial arrangements for parish and town councils more responsive to the current needs and future aspirations of those councils – particularly the larger ones – and of the people who use and pay for the services which they provide.

6.18   Chapter 9 of part II describes a package of finance measures for parishes. Some of them will benefit all parishes, whereas a few are intended specifically to meet the needs of the larger ones. The key measures include:

- paying a grant of £30,000 per year to each best value parish, when legislation permits (see chapter 3);

- improving the borrowing approval system by removing the annual fixed limit, streamlining the application process and by clarifying and advertising the criteria more widely;

- increasing the ceiling on 'section 137' expenditure (expenditure of general benefit to the area, on activities for which specific powers do not exist) to £5 per elector and then raising it annually in line with inflation; and

- encouraging good practice in establishing funding arrangements when parishes work in partnership with principal authorities (for example by taking on responsibility for providing some local services). We are working to produce a set of guidelines with the National Association of Local Councils and the Local Government Association (LGA).

The challenge for councils

6.19   This white paper sets out what the Government will do to promote better services and community leadership by enhancing local freedom and responsibility. Success will require a matching effort from councils. Good financial management will be one of the keys to success.

6.20   The best authorities plan ahead. They have clear long-term objectives, which drive their spending plans. Their capital investment strategies are based on a sound assessment of the condition of their assets. Their council tax, charging and revenue spending plans are based on proper consultation with local people about their willingness to pay for better services. They have good internal systems for monitoring spend and delivery. They are serious about increasing their spending power by improving efficiency. They set prudent levels of reserves. They share the benefits of the greater predictability and stability on funding: schools have indicative budgets for future years; voluntary sector bodies don't have to bid for funds annually; council tax decisions do not take local people by surprise. Members are actively involved at every stage. The executive takes full responsibility for setting objectives and budgets, including the tough decisions on priorities that are an inevitable part of the budget-setting process in any organisation. Overview and scrutiny committees challenge budgets and monitor spending, delivery and efficiency.

6.21   We want to see all local authorities bring their financial management arrangements in line with this best practice. We will introduce legislation to reinforce the role of members in setting and monitoring budgets. We shall work with the LGA on guidance for public consultation. We will ensure that the Audit Commission's comprehensive performance assessments take account of whether authorities are following best practice in all aspects of planning and managing their finances (see chapter 3).

6.22   We believe that the greater financial freedom and responsibility we are offering local government, backed up by good local financial management, will reinforce local democracy and improve service delivery.

CHAPTER 7
Working together for better outcomes

The proposals in this white paper will transform relations between central and local government.

Old-fashioned, top-down approaches will be replaced by clear standards, jointly agreed priorities, and effective systems to secure their delivery.

The clutter of current controls and regulations will be replaced by streamlined, better targeted and more effective approaches which:

- recognise and reward good performance;
- encourage improvement; and
- trigger tough action on failure.

Effective and practical arrangements at national level will support this partnership between central and local government.

Transforming the relationship between central and local government

7.1   Central and local government have a common interest: improving people's quality of life. The ability of local government to play its part in this joint endeavour is affected, in part, by the way in which central government seeks to influence its actions. In the past, too little importance has been attached to this relationship, and how well it works. We have successfully addressed this shortcoming at national level, with the establishment of the Central Local Partnership.

7.2   The challenge for the future is to transform Government's relationship with individual councils. In some instances this works well. In others it does not. Across all Departments, Government needs to move away from a fragmented and uncoordinated approach to a partnership based on clear standards, common priorities, greater freedoms for councils to deliver, and effective action where they do not.

7.3   The proposals set out in this white paper signal a major shift in this direction. A start has already been made, with the introduction of innovative schemes such as local Public Service Agreements (PSA). Further steps will follow. Progress will depend on effective joint working between central and local government – a genuine central local partnership. The prize for success will be faster progress towards our joint goal – providing a better quality of life for everyone.

7.4   The Government recognises the distinctive roles to be played by different types of local authority: upper-tier councils, district councils and parish and town councils. The vast majority of proposals in this white paper apply equally to all principal authorities: county councils, unitaries, metropolitan and London boroughs and shire districts. The exceptions are in our approach to local PSAs and the timing of comprehensive performance assessments. The box summarises our approach for district councils in these two areas and describes our approach for parish and town councils.

Our approach for district, parish and town councils

Shire district councils

The large majority of proposals in this white paper apply to both upper tier and shire district councils. The exceptions are the approach to local PSAs and the timing of comprehensive performance assessments.

Local PSAs are being extended to all upper tier councils (on a voluntary basis). The Government recognises the importance of district councils and believes that the way forward is for districts to work in collaboration with upper tier councils on local PSAs. Chapter 3 underlines this by providing for:

- strong encouragement for county councils' local PSAs to include targets that require collaboration with districts;

- a larger potential reward grant where there is substantial district involvement (reflecting the budgets of participating districts as well as counties); and

- a larger pump priming grant in recognition of the extra administrative costs of negotiating the involvement of districts.

In chapter 5 we encourage district councils to make use of the Improvement and Development Agency Local Government Improvement Programme before they have their comprehensive performance assessments. This will help them make more effective use of their resources for support by identifying and targeting weaknesses.

We will also make council tax bills more transparent, so that taxpayers can see by how much different authorities (e.g. county, district and parish) are increasing their council tax.

Parish and town councils

Town and parish councils have an important contribution to make to local well-being. That is why the recent Rural White Paper[1] and subsequent consultation document[2] does much to augment the position of town and parish councils, through initiatives such as:

- a Town and Parish Council Charter;

- the Quality Parish scheme which will allow qualifying town and parish councils to take on new and wider responsibilities; and

- new funding to assist town and parish councils to play a fuller role in their communities.

In addition to these measures, this white paper proposes:

- separate guidance for town and parish councils which will include the streamlining measures set out elsewhere in this white paper;

- guidance to principal authorities advising them to include in their Best Value Performance Plans their arrangements for working in partnership with parishes on neighbourhood service delivery;

- when legislation permits, a grant of £30,000 each year to best value parishes to cover the costs of audit and carrying out best value related work such as the preparation of performance plans and the management of reviews; and

- a package of finance measures for parishes, some aimed at all parishes and a few intended specifically to meet the needs of the larger ones. The key measures include:

  - improving the borrowing approval system by removing the annual fixed limit, streamlining the application process and by clarifying and advertising the criteria more widely;

  - increasing the ceiling on 'section 137' expenditure (expenditure of general benefit to the area, on activities for which specific powers do not exist) to £5 per elector and then raising it annually in line with inflation; and

  - encouraging good practice in establishing funding arrangements when parishes work in partnership with principal authorities (for example by taking on responsibility for providing some local services). We are working to produce a set of guidelines with the National Association of Local Councils and the Local Government Association.

---

[1] *Our Countryside: The Future A Fair Deal for Rural England* – DETR, MAFF, November 2000, Cm 4909, ISBN 0101490925. http://www.defra.gov.uk/erdp/erdpfrm.htm

[2] *Quality Parish and Town Councils: A Consultation Paper*, DEFRA, DTLR, NALC, LGA, Countryside Agency, November 2001 http://www.defra.gov.uk/wildlife-countryside/consult/qtpc/index.htm

7.5   As we said in our manifesto, we also believe that there can be an important role for directly elected assemblies for the English regions. Regional assemblies would be strategic, help join-up strategies and policies at regional level and give the regions a new political voice and a stronger identity. They would work closely with local authorities and complement their roles. The Government's proposals for regional government will be set out in a white paper to be published next year.

The future of the Central Local Partnership

7.6   In November 1997 the Government and the newly-formed Local Government Association (LGA) signed a Framework for Partnership. This was a significant step forward from the ad hoc and unsatisfactory arrangements that had existed previously. The Framework provided the basis for an effective and practical Central Local Partnership (CLP).

7.7   Through the CLP, central and local government have been able to develop a sound understanding of each other's position across the whole range of domestic policy issues. More importantly, the CLP has been the platform on which real joint work has taken place – to help to tackle social exclusion, address the challenges of rural areas and help the country to prepare better for incidents of severe weather, to name only a few activities.

7.8   The CLP will continue to be the centrepiece of national relations between central and local government. The Framework Agreement signed in 1997 by the Deputy Prime Minister and the Chairman of the LGA provides the basis for the overall conduct of central local relations. It will be revised and updated to reflect developments since 1997, including the principles set out in this white paper.

Setting priorities

7.9   Chapter 3 describes our proposal to identify priorities for local government through the CLP framework. As the LGA has suggested[3], these priorities will draw on the Government's top priorities and incorporate wider priorities identified by local government such as the LGA's six priorities for public service delivery. The priorities will be endorsed at a meeting of the CLP. They will inform the national PSA for local government and be used by each council in the development of their local PSA to marry nationally-agreed priorities with locally identified ones.

7.10   The Secretary of State for Transport, Local Government and the Regions will make the priorities for local government available to Parliament as soon as possible. It will, of course, be a matter for Parliament itself to decide what further scrutiny should be given to them. Select Committees of the House of Commons may wish to look at elements of the priorities relating to policy areas within their own remit, or to work together in scrutinising cross-cutting commitments.

Delivering and evaluating progress

7.11   Implementing the proposals in this white paper requires a corporate approach by Government in support of the new performance framework. We need to ensure that there is the necessary co-ordination and capacity within and

---

[3] *Partnership for Ambition: councils and government working together* LGA Paper, November 2001. http://www.lga.gov.uk/lga/clp/ambition.htm

between Departments, the inspectorates, and the agencies which support the modernisation of local government. Reporting to the Secretary of State, the Department for Transport, Local Government and the Regions (DTLR) and the Office of Public Services Reform will work together to develop an implementation plan and suitable monitoring arrangements to deliver this new approach.

7.12 We will monitor and evaluate the effectiveness and impact of the policies and programmes set out in this white paper as part of our commitment to evaluation of the overall local government modernisation agenda. Information about policy evaluations, along with other local government research commissioned by the DTLR, can be found on the website at: http://www.local.dtlr.gov.uk/research/index.htm.

A practical partnership for change

7.13 A new, more mature partnership between central and local government must have at its heart a single aim – to give people everywhere the opportunities they need to make their lives better. This white paper sets out a radical agenda for doing this. People will benefit from the assurance that all services will improve and be delivered to acceptable standards. They will benefit from a focus on what really matters to them. And they will benefit from having their council listen to, and stand up for, their needs and aspirations. Together, local and central government can help achieve better outcomes for everyone. The people we serve expect and deserve no less.

CONTENTS: PART II

CHAPTER 1
Aims and priorities

The starting point

1.1   Part one of the white paper sets out a comprehensive and radical reform agenda for local government. In this second part, we set out in more depth our specific proposals for reform of the local government finance system.

1.2   In 1997, local government in England was in trouble. There were wide variations in quality of service, turnout at local elections was low and declining, and there was a general lack of interest in local authorities. In 1998, we addressed these problems in *Modern Local Government – In Touch with the People*, and we acted during the remainder of the last Parliament to implement its proposals. We gave local authorities a general power to promote the well-being of communities. We introduced the duty of best value, backed up by audit and inspection, to raise standards across the board. We introduced beacon councils to spread best practice. We introduced new political structures, in which executive and scrutiny responsibilities are clearly separated, backed up by a new ethical framework.

1.3   On the finance side, our focus during the last Parliament was on increasing funding for local government, and delivering greater predictability and stability. Between 1994-95 and 1997-98, revenue grant declined in real terms, but it is now increasing by nearly 5 per cent a year. Government support for local government capital investment was declining even more sharply, but is now increasing by over 20 per cent a year. The introduction of two-yearly spending reviews and the freeze on changes to the revenue grant formulae have made it easier for local authorities to plan ahead. The abolition of 'crude and universal' capping started the process of removing oppressive Government controls over local authorities. However, *Modern Local Government – In Touch with the People* recognised the need for more

radical reform of the finance system. In September last year, we published *Modernising Local Government Finance: A Green Paper*.

What the green paper said

1.4   The green paper set out nine aims of a good local government finance system. It should fund all authorities adequately. It should promote continuous improvement in service quality and efficiency. It should provide a reasonable degree of predictability and stability. It should balance delivery of national priorities and targets with local financial freedom and responsibility. It should be fair to those who use and pay for local authority services. It should clarify accountability for financial decisions. It should be intelligible and transparent to all stakeholders. It should facilitate partnership working. It should encourage consultation.

1.5   The green paper concluded that the existing system does not meet these aims well. Revenue grant is not allocated fairly. There are still too many Government controls. The system is too complicated, and is not well understood by people in local government, let alone by those they serve. This reduces transparency and undermines accountability.

What you said

1.6   Very few respondents to the green paper challenged any of these aims. Comments tended to focus on their emphasis and their relative importance.

1.7   Respondents welcomed the increase in funding for local government and the steps to improve predictability and stability, but they agreed with the Government that there was a need to go further. Local authorities attached particular importance to local financial autonomy. Some believed that local financial freedom and responsibility required a shift in the balance of funding, with a reduction in Government grant and an increase in local taxes. Others focused more on the importance of reducing the number of Government-imposed controls on how local authorities raise money and on how they spend it.

1.8 There was general acceptance of the need to reform grant formulae, although there were differing views on when and how this should be done. Respondents recognised the need to make the system more intelligible, as well as tackling its unfairnesses.

The Government's approach

1.9 The Government believes that the aims set out in the local government finance green paper are the right ones. We also believe that all the aims are important. We are therefore committed to securing a reformed local government finance system, which meets all of these aims better than the present system does.

1.10 However, as we stressed in the green paper, finance issues cannot be viewed in isolation. A good finance system is a means to an end, not an end in its own right. Over the next five years, the Government's top priority is to secure improvements in delivery across the whole range of public services, but with a particular emphasis on tackling crime and improving education, health and transport. Local government has a key role to play here. Even in those areas where local authorities act primarily as agents of central government in the delivery of national priorities, they cannot discharge that role properly if they are over-constrained by Government. And we are clear that local authorities' have a role which extends well beyond delivery of national priorities. They

are a separate tier of government, answerable to local voters and taxpayers, with local priorities to pursue and a local community leadership responsibility to discharge.

1.11 The aims set out in the local government finance green paper are consistent with the broader reform agenda mapped out in part one of this document. However, we have reviewed the specific proposals in the green paper. Our main conclusions are that the local government finance reform agenda needs to be more radical and more discriminating in terms of financial freedom, that change needs to be carefully managed, and that more needs to be done to promote good local financial management in which councillors are fully involved.

A more radical reform agenda

1.12 The green paper proposed that we should abolish the requirement that local authorities seek government approval before borrowing for capital investment, extend authorities' freedom to charge for discretionary services and give local authorities limited freedom to vary the business rate in their areas. We shall implement the first two of these proposals, and on the third we shall enable authorities to explore with local businesses the scope for targeted and additional investment in business improvement districts (BIDs).

1.13 In addition, we intend to introduce a number of reforms for all authorities which give them greater control over how they raise, spend and invest their money, and which reduce bureaucracy. The key proposals here include action on ring-fenced grants and the abolition of the council tax subsidy limitation scheme and the 'receipts taken into account' mechanism. We are also consulting on the introduction of local authority discretion over council tax discounts and exemptions and a relaxation of the rules on local authorities' general fund investments.

A more discriminating agenda

1.14   Local authorities vary, in terms of the quality of service they deliver and their capacity to improve. The white paper proposes a classification of authorities into four groups:

- *high-performing* – near the top of the performance spectrum with high performance in priority service areas, no poorly performing services and with proven capacity to improve;

- *striving* – not necessarily at the top of the performance spectrum but with proven capacity to improve;

- *coasting* – not at the top of the performance spectrum and with limited or no proven capacity to improve;

- *poor-performing* – consistently near the bottom of the performance spectrum and with limited or no proven capacity to improve.

Chapter 3 in part I of this white paper explains how the Audit Commission will make this classification, which will include a corporate governance assessment in which the strength of authorities' financial management will be an important consideration.

1.15   The freedoms and responsibilities in paragraphs 1.12 and 1.13 will be available to all authorities. In addition, *high-performing* authorities will secure the following freedoms as of right, whilst *striving* authorities will have access to them via the local PSA:

- the right to have any grant paid, other than that which must be passed on to schools, as targeted grant rather than ring-fenced grant, which means that there will be no Government-imposed conditions on how the funds are spent;

- freedom to trade across all services;

- greater freedom to use income from fines.

These financial freedoms supplement the lighter touch inspection regime, greater discretion in designing their own programme of best value reviews and the further reduction in plan-production requirements from which these authorities will also benefit.

1.16   Poorly performing authorities present particular difficulties. We do not want to aggravate their problems by imposing financial penalties or taking resources away from them. The intention is to reward and incentivise success, not to penalise failure, particularly since taking resources away from poor performing authorities penalises users of local services and local taxpayers. But poor performers need to focus their efforts on the key task of improving services and strengthening corporate management; it is not helpful or appropriate for them to divert effort onto additional activities, such as trading. And we are fully prepared to take freedoms, such as the new borrowing freedoms or increased financial flexibility, away from authorities that prove incapable of exercising them responsibly.

Managing change

1.17   Changes to the local government finance system can be disruptive. Even though a change is eminently justified and produces a fairer outcome at the national level, it may still have an adverse and unfair impact on individual authorities or other stakeholders. We are committed to managing individual changes to the finance system to minimise these adverse impacts. Transitional relief will prevent revaluation having an excessive impact on business rate or council tax bills. Floors and ceilings will provide authorities with protection from volatility in the data used in the grant formulae. But we also need to ensure that the change agenda as a whole is managed sensibly.

1.18   In deciding the sequence in which we will tackle the different elements of the local government finance reform agenda, we have asked three questions about each proposal:

- How does it contribute to the overarching goal of securing the delivery of better services – meeting national targets, addressing local priorities, and improving cost-effectiveness?

- To what extent might it actually disrupt or distract from delivery of better services?

- How does it link to other elements in the local government finance reform agenda?

1.19   Many of the reforms proposed in this paper have very little impact on local authorities' delivery of better front-line services. Examples include reform of the business rate transitional relief scheme, introducing greater clarity into council tax bills, establishing the administrative support for valuation tribunals as a non-departmental public body. These free-standing reforms can proceed to their own timetables. However, there are three groups of reforms which will have a significant impact on service delivery.

1.20   The first group comprises reforms to the **revenue grant system**. Securing adequate funding is a necessary condition for the delivery of service improvement. We cannot persevere with a grant system which replicates past patterns of spend rather than allocating grant

where it is most needed and will do most good. But, whilst reform of the grant system is an urgent priority, we must ensure that there is adequate time for preparation and consultation. We have therefore decided to keep the existing grant distribution formula stable for 2002-03 and frame new grant formulae, in partnership with local government, which will distribute formula grant for 2003-04. We shall then reintroduce the 'freeze' on formula changes for 2004-05 and 2005-06. In addition, we need to shift the balance between ring-fenced and general grant, and find ways of securing delivery of national objectives which do not undermine local authorities' ability to meet local priorities.

1.21   The second group of reforms gives greater **local freedom and responsibility,** and will help promote action to meet local priorities. The reforms include giving authorities freedom to borrow without Government consent, introducing business improvement districts and giving councils greater freedom to set fees and charges, plus many other more modest reforms. We shall implement all of these reforms during this Parliament. If they were all implemented in parallel with one another and with the changes to the grant formulae, they could be disruptive and could overstrain local authority finance departments. However, these changes require legislation. We shall introduce a Bill as soon as the parliamentary timetable permits. Our hope is that this timetable will allow the reforms to be implemented shortly after the process of introducing the new revenue grant system has been completed.

1.22   The third group of changes relate to **council tax**. A council tax revaluation cannot be deferred indefinitely. However, we believe that the combined effect of a council tax revaluation and the other reforms in this white paper – particularly the introduction of a new grant system – would be too disruptive. Inevitably, some council taxpayers would find that their bills were affected quite substantially by both changes. There will therefore be no council tax revaluation in this Parliament, but we shall introduce legislation which provides for a revaluation, with new bands being reflected in 2007 bills. Ahead of revaluation, we will listen to the views of taxpayers and local government about council tax bands and related matters. We shall introduce legislation to make it clear that additional council tax valuation bands can be created without new primary legislation.

Strengthening local financial management

1.23   This paper sets out what the Government will do to promote better services by enhancing local freedom and responsibility. But success will require a matching effort from councils. And good financial management will be one of the keys to success.

1.24   We shall ensure that the corporate assessment of the authority takes account of its financial performance. We shall introduce legislation to reinforce the role of members, creating new duties to maintain adequate reserves and to keep finances under review during the financial year. The new borrowing freedoms will require all authorities to do effective forward planning, including preparing revenue forecasts looking at least three years ahead, to set alongside their forward capital strategies. But good financial management is not something that Government can legislate or regulate for. At the end of the day it is for elected members, supported by good quality advice and sound management by officers, to ensure that their financial management systems and decision making processes are robust and that the resources available to the authority are used efficiently and effectively.

Working together

1.25   As the remaining chapters show, the proposals in the rest of this paper reflect extensive consultation and joint working with local government and other stakeholders. The consultations that followed the publication of the green paper have substantially informed our proposals for reforming local government finance. An important purpose of this second part of the white paper is to provide a detailed response to the issues raised by consultees and to show how their views have shaped policy. But joint working has by no means been confined to the formal green paper consultation process. In particular, on the revenue side the green paper was heavily informed by the review of revenue grant distribution undertaken jointly by central and local government; and the proposed new prudential regime was developed by a working group consisting of representatives from relevant Government Departments, the Local Government Association, CIPFA and the Audit Commission. Both of these reviews were initiated under the auspices of the central/local partnership. Since the green paper was published, joint working has continued in these and other areas. We will continue to work closely with local government and other key stakeholders in implementing the proposals set out in the rest of this paper.

CHAPTER 2

The balance of funding and the balance of control

The starting point

2.1   Up until 1990, local taxes (the domestic and non-domestic rates) accounted for over 50 per cent of local authority revenue, and national taxes accounted for less than 50 per cent. The nationalisation of the business rate in 1990 shifted the balance of funding so that the proportion of local authority revenue funded by local taxes reduced from about 50 per cent to 25 per cent. National taxes (including the business rate) now account for about 75 per cent of local authority revenue and local taxes for about 25 per cent.

2.2   The period since 1990 has seen many other changes in the relationship between central and local government. In 1990, the previous administration considerably tightened Government controls on capital spending. In 1984, and more widely in 1993, it took powers to cap local authorities' council tax increases. The use of these powers increasingly took the form of 'crude and universal' capping, under which the Government announced in advance the maximum budget increase that it was prepared to permit.

2.3   Under this administration, 'crude and universal' capping has been abolished, and the principle that the council tax increase is a matter for local decision has been re-established. However, in order to carry out its policy aims, this Government has also pursued a more interventionist approach to how Government funding is spent. On the revenue side, ring-fenced grant has increased much more rapidly than general grant. On the capital finance side, support provided in the form of supplementary credit approvals and ring-fenced grants has increased more rapidly than basic credit approvals.

What the green paper said

2.4   The green paper stressed the need for greater local freedom and responsibility. It made specific proposals to enhance local decision-making – on borrowing, on a supplement to the business rate, and on fees and charges. However, it did not see a case for shifting the balance of funding.

2.5   The green paper set out options for a new funding regime for education. These included approaches which involved ring-fencing all education spend. However, the Government made clear that its preferred approach was to retain local freedom to determine how much was spent on education and how funds were allocated between schools, whilst introducing much greater transparency into the funding system. This would be achieved by separating schools and non-schools funding for local authorities, and also by establishing within the grant formula for schools a pupil entitlement. The effect would be to permit local stakeholders to track funding from the decisions taken by Government in the spending review through to the setting of the budget for the individual school.

What you said

2.6   Most respondents welcomed the abolition of 'crude and universal' capping, and welcomed the other freedoms in the green paper. There was concern about the growth of ring-fenced grant. And, as noted in chapter 1, some respondents believed that local financial freedom and responsibility required a shift in the balance of funding, with a reduction in Government grant and an increase in local taxes. Some argued that the European Charter on Local Self-Government required such a shift in the balance of funding. The Local Government Association (LGA) suggested we set up a commission to investigate the whole question of local financial autonomy.

2.7   There was a wide range of views on education funding. Many schools remain concerned that the increased funding which we are providing is not reaching them, and would prefer to see Government grant for schools wholly ring-fenced. Some councils feared that, by identifying separately schools and non-schools funding, the Government would erode local authority freedom to set spending priorities. In general, respondents thought that the proposed approach struck a sensible balance, and welcomed the greater transparency it would bring.

The Government's approach

2.8   We do not think there are any quick or easy ways of securing a major shift in the balance of funding. However, we need to be clear what the longer-term reform options are and whether there are more modest reform options that could be pursued more quickly. We will explore the options with local government (see paragraphs 2.16–2.17).

2.9   We believe that the balance of control is a more pressing issue than the balance of funding. The Government is convinced that too much decision-making responsibility has become centralised in Whitehall. The combination of Government control over authorities' revenue budgets (via 'crude and universal' capping) and over their capital spend (via credit approvals) virtually eliminated local financial discretion, other than the freedom to set their own spending priorities within a Government-determined total. We have already abolished 'crude and universal' capping. We are now committed to abolishing credit approvals, too. The question is: What more needs to be done?

2.10   Ring-fencing is one of the principle constraints on local freedom to manoeuvre. It erodes local authorities' ability to respond to local priorities and drives up council tax increases. We shall therefore restrict ring-fencing to cases which are genuine high priorities for Government and where we cannot achieve our policy goal by specifying output or outcome targets (see paragraphs 2.21–2.25).

2.11   We shall reform the funding of education along the lines set out in the green paper, introducing much greater transparency into the budget setting process at all levels. Stakeholders will be able to track the pupil entitlement, on which the new grant formula for schools will be based, from the spending review outcome through to the setting of a budget for an individual school.

THE BALANCE OF FUNDING

2.12   We have reviewed this question on three separate occasions – when producing the 1998 white paper, when responding to the Environment, Transport and Regional Affairs Committee's report *Local Government Finance* and again in preparing this white paper. On each occasion, we have concluded that the balance of funding and the balance of control are separate issues.

2.13   The table below shows the balance of funding in the budgets which local authorities have set for the current financial year in England. In round terms, Government grant (including the reallocated proceeds of the business rate) accounts for three-quarters of local government revenue spend, whilst council tax accounts for one-quarter. The proportions have not changed significantly in recent years.

2.14   Although it is often argued that the current balance between national and local taxes has an adverse impact on local authorities' autonomy, there is little hard evidence for or against this view, and there is no consensus on how the balance might be shifted.

Budgets for 2001-02	(£bn)	(%)	General grant =	(£bn)	(%)
General grant	40.247	65.7%	Revenue support grant	21.086	34.4%
Ring-fenced grant	5.292	8.6%	SSA reduction grant & CSPG	0.003	0.0%
Government grant	45.539	74.3%	Police grant	3.798	6.2%
Council tax	15.244	24.9%	Business rates	15.137	24.7%
Reserves	0.479	0.8%	Neighbourhood Renewal Fund	0.200	0.3%
Local resources	15.723	25.7%	General GLA grant	0.023	0.0%
Total	61.262	100.0%	Total	40.247	65.7%

2.15   The main reason why local authorities are concerned about the balance of funding is its impact on their 'gearing'. For an authority which gets three-quarters of its funding from Government, a 1 per cent increase in budget requires a 4 per cent increase in council tax. If the authority had a lower gearing, it would be able to increase its spending more painlessly. The Government's comments on gearing are:

- The gearing effect has some advantages. In particular, it encourages authorities to look for ways of increasing their spending power by driving down costs, rather than pushing up taxes.

- Gearing created real problems when authorities faced grant cuts or increases well below what was needed to maintain existing services. But, as a result of the increased grant provided by this Government and the introduction of floors and ceilings, no authority should find itself in that position today.

- There is no obviously 'right' level of gearing for local authorities. Even if there were a 'right' level of gearing, it would be impossible to get all local authorities in England to it. Some authorities will always need more grant than others, because their taxbase is smaller or because the cost of providing services in their area is higher.

2.16   Once we have done some further analysis, we shall establish a high-level working group, involving Ministers and senior figures from local government, to look at all aspects of the balance of funding, reviewing the evidence and looking at reform options.

2.17   We do not think there are any quick or easy ways of securing a major shift in the balance of funding, particularly given the need to respect the views of taxpayers and to ensure that financial reform does not become a distraction from the delivery agenda. However, we need to be clear what the longer-term reform options are. We also need to consider whether there are more modest reform options that could be pursued more quickly.

THE BALANCE OF CONTROL

2.18   In the Government's view, the balance of control is a more serious and urgent issue than the balance of funding.

2.19   We have stressed in chapter 1 that our priority for this Parliament is the delivery of better services. We believe that the public shares our view of the areas where there is a nation-wide need for better services – raising educational standards, improving the quality of the nation's health, reducing crime and the fear of crime, etc. However, it is clear that people also want to see some action on local priorities – dealing with run-down town centres and housing estates, cleaning up graffiti, dog-mess and litter, making streets and open spaces safer, etc. In return for the large investment that they are making in local authority services, taxpayers are entitled to see progress on both fronts. It is therefore an important aim of a good local government finance system that it allows local authorities to meet both national and local priorities.

2.20   The Government has acted to increase local financial freedom by abolishing 'crude and universal' capping. Many of the proposals in this white paper are intended to give local authorities greater freedom to respond to local priorities. The capital finance reforms, business improvement districts, freedom to set fees and charges, and greater freedom to retain and reinvest the income from fines are all cases in point. However, we also need to find ways of balancing the calls of national and local priorities on authorities' revenue budgets.

RING-FENCED GRANT

2.21   When we took office in 1997, ring-fenced grant accounted for 5 per cent of all Government grant to local authorities. In 2001-02, it accounts for 12 per cent of all grant. The 2000 spending review planned for a further increase to 15 per cent by 2003-04.

2.22   Ring-fencing remains an important means of bringing about change; for example, ensuring that councils and schools direct sufficient attention to areas that have been neglected in the past. Nevertheless, the growth in ring-fencing is a source of concern to central and local government, because ring-fenced grants can create other problems. They can erode authorities' discretion to vary their spending priorities to fit local circumstances. They can have a high transaction cost, particularly where securing the grant depends on the preparation of plans or bids. They can also get in the way of partnership working and local initiative. The new

performance framework in the white paper will allow us to take a more outcome focused approach to delivery which will make ring-fenced funding less necessary.

2.23   The Government has undertaken a review of all ring-fenced grants to local authorities. Some ring-fencing clearly makes sense and is welcomed by local authorities generally. However, the measures outlined in this chapter will place responsibility for decisions on local funding needs firmly back in the hands of those who, in the Government view, are best placed to take those decisions: local authorities. Cost unevenness can be dealt with through targeted grants; the ring-fenced grant should be restricted to areas where local government cannot be relied on to devote sufficient effort in a particular area – e.g. for benefits that accrue to others. Through the spending reviews, we will vet all proposals for new ring-fenced grants to ensure that they meet our key tests:

- there are good reasons why the Government should require local authorities to spend the funds on a specific purpose;

- we have to target inputs, rather than the outcomes/outputs we want to achieve;

- there should be an exit strategy;

- the service covered by the ring-fenced grant must be a genuine Government priority; and

- there will be no match funding other than for very small pilot schemes.

2.24   We will keep all ring-fencing under review, with the aim of removing it as soon as it is possible to do so. We shall vet proposals for new and continuing ring-fenced grants through the spending review process, to ensure that over time all ring-fencing is consistent with our tests. As the funding arrangements for the police are somewhat different, any specific funding issues for police authorities will be dealt with outside the above arrangements.

2.25   High-performing authorities (i.e. those who are near the top of the performance spectrum with high-performance in priority service areas, no poorly performing services and with a proven capacity to improve) have shown their commitment to achieving the Government's objectives. In return, such authorities deserve a special measure of trust, and we will therefore give them the right to have ring-fenced grant replaced by targeted grant in any case where they judge it to be desirable, except in respect of grants which have to be passed to schools. This is over and above such freedoms as the authorities may agree through their local PSAs as described in chapter 3. Reducing ring-fencing is consistent with our aim in this white paper to give councils more space to innovate, to respond in ways that are appropriate to local circumstances and to provide more effective leadership.

Funding education

2.26   In some key areas, such as education, the Government has exercised much tighter control over local authority activities than previous administrations. To do so was appropriate in the circumstances. Improving the quality of children's education is an important goal in its own right. It also makes a vital contribution to national economic and social agendas. Our focus has been primarily on outputs and outcomes. We have set challenging targets for improvements in GCSE passes, Key Stage test results, and numeracy and literacy. But we have also taken a close interest in how services are delivered and how money is spent. The box sets out some of the ways in which the Government has intervened to influence local authority spending on education, and the reasons why this has been necessary.

Influencing education spending

The Government has a Manifesto commitment to increase education spend as a proportion of national income. We cannot honour this commitment unless local authorities increase their spend on education in line with the increase in education SSA. The Secretary of State for Education and Skills has written to councils urging them to do this.

We are keen to ensure that the grant we provide reaches schools and other front-line service providers. The Government has set targets for the proportion of authorities' education budgets which is devoted to schools. We have publicised cases where authorities have not met the targets.

There are areas of activity which have been neglected in the past. They include raising standards of numeracy and literacy, the teaching of music and other specialist subjects and the professional development of teachers. The use of ring-fenced funding has helped ensure that these areas receive proper attention in schools.

2.27   In education, the tension between meeting national objectives and delivering local priorities has been particularly acute. Local authorities have argued that the pressure we put on them to increase their spend on education in line with our increase in education SSA can leave them with a choice between steep council tax increases or cuts to other services. However, now that we have put the right framework in place, with the commitment to new ways of working, there can be less central determination and greater local decision making. We believe that the new grant system for education provides a solution to this problem.

2.28   The Government has concluded that it should continue to provide the majority of its support for education in the form of general grant. We shall not therefore ring-fence all funding for education. Nor shall we remove local authorities' discretion to set budgets at the local level. However, we shall monitor how the new system works and we will have a reserve power, in exceptional circumstances, to direct a local authority to set a budget for expenditure on schools at no less than a level determined by the Secretary of State having regard to all relevant circumstances.

2.29 The new funding regime will distinguish clearly between funding intended for schools and funding intended for other responsibilities of a local education authority. The schools formula will be based on a pupil entitlement, plus an enhancement for authorities with deprivation problems and an enhancement for authorities which face high costs of recruiting and retaining staff. The pupil entitlement is an entitlement to a level of expenditure, rather than an entitlement to an amount of grant from Government. One important advantage of this approach is that it makes it much easier for key stakeholders – governors, heads, teachers and parents – to track funding through the system, from the outcome of the spending review to the setting of the budget for an individual school.

Tracking funding through the system

Step 1: The Government announces at the end of the spending review a new indicative pupil entitlement of £P for every primary school pupil in England.

Step 2: The local authority sets its council tax and its total budget for all services.

Step 3: The authority allocates its total budget between education and other services.

Step 4: The authority divides its education budget into budgets for primary schools, secondary schools and other education spend. Other things being equal, an authority with 5,000 primary school pupils should set a budget for primary schools of 5,000 x £P.

Step 5: The authority allocates the budget for primary schools between the individual schools, using the locally agreed fair funding formula. The average primary school with 200 pupils should get a budget of 200 x £P, though this will vary according to schools' circumstances.

2.30 The box shows how funding for primary school pupils can be tracked in this way. It assumes (for the sake of simplicity) that the authority gets no deprivation or pay enhancement. The governors, head, teachers and parents of an individual school will start by looking at the budget they get from the authority. A school with 200 pupils would get on average a budget of 200 times the pupil entitlement. If it gets a very different figure, it will want to find out why. It may be that the budget set for all primary schools is in line with the national pupil entitlement, but the local fair funding formula gives some schools much more than others. Or the explanation may lie further back at steps 2, 3 or 4.

2.31 The aim behind the new system is that the authority should have discretion to take the decisions it thinks right, in the light of local circumstances, at each of steps 2 to 5. But it should explain clearly the reasons for the decisions it takes at each step, so that schools understand them and can challenge them if they are dissatisfied. It should also involve its stakeholders. It should consult schools on steps 4 and 5, in the same way that it should consult local people generally on steps 2 and 3 (see chapter 6).

2.32 Because the new system is more transparent and subjects local authority decisions to closer local scrutiny, it reduces the need for Government to press local authorities on the overall level of education spending or on the split between schools and non-schools funding. We shall need to keep the working of the new grant system under review. If it works as we hope and expect, it should meet the Government's concerns about how education funds are spent, with less intervention from Ministers.

CHAPTER 3
The way forward on general grant

The starting point

3.1   The Government has traditionally provided two main types of grant to local authorities – general grant and ring-fenced grant. Ring-fenced grant can only be spent for the specific purpose for which it is provided. General grant can be used to fund any activity of a local authority.

3.2   The revenue grant distribution system allocates £40 billion of general grant between 432 authorities, with widely differing local circumstances. It covers police and fire authorities, counties and shire districts, and all-purpose authorities. It covers inner cities, suburbs, small towns and sparsely populated rural areas. It covers prosperous and deprived areas.

3.3   General grant is distributed between these authorities using a complex set of formulae, based on the 'standard spending assessment' (SSA). The policing SSA uses the same formula as that for police grant, which reflects the policing responsibilities of the Home Office. The aim behind the formulae is to reflect variations in the cost of providing services and variations in the amount of council tax that different authorities can raise. The SSA system has been in place for the last ten years. Similar systems have been in use since the mid-1970s.

3.4   Neither the Government nor local authorities have great confidence in the SSA system. An extensive attitude survey carried out in 1999 showed that most people in local government did not think they understood the SSA system and had reservations about its fairness.

What the green paper said

3.5   The green paper said that formulae could continue to play a role in distributing grant, but highlighted some of the weaknesses of the SSA system and stressed that any formula-based system was bound to have limitations. It suggested two ways of supplementing formulae. One approach would be for the grant decision to take account of local authorities' own corporate plans, which will reflect local spending pressures and ambitions. Targeted grants can be used to target resources at authorities with additional spending pressures, without recourse to ring-fencing. Local PSAs provide financial and other incentives to improve service delivery.

3.6   The green paper stressed the importance of predictability and stability. It suggested that floors and ceilings should be introduced to ensure that the grant increases which the formulae produce for individual authorities would be kept within a predictable range. It suggested that formula freezes might become a permanent feature of the grant system: instead of being updated annually, formulae would be revised every two or four years (to align with the spending review cycle). It also sought views on whether to extend the existing three-year formula freeze to cover 2002-03.

What you said

3.7   Most local authorities thought that formulae were an important element in a general grant distribution system, but agreed that it was not sensible to rely wholly on formulae.

3.8   The majority of authorities were opposed to taking councils' own corporate plans into account in the grant decision. The main concern about this approach was that it involved Ministers taking a view on authorities' spending plans. Respondents feared that this could undermine local democratic accountability.

3.9 Respondents welcomed the steps the Government has already taken to deliver greater predictability and stability. Most respondents supported the introduction of floors and ceilings, and agreed that formula freezes should be a permanent feature of the general grant distribution system. Whilst there was general support for the new approach from both schools and local authorities, there were strongly divergent views on the case for extending the current SSA formula freeze. Schools wanted to see the new approach to distributing funds for education introduced from 2002-03; the majority of local authorities, on the other hand, felt that introduction before 2003-04 would not be practical.

The Government's approach

3.10 The Government believes that the reform of the general grant system is an urgent priority. We are already providing local authorities with the financial support to deliver continuous improvement in service quality and efficiency through increases in Government grant and support for capital investment. This will be reinforced by introducing a fairer and more stable revenue grant distribution system which puts money where it is needed and will do most good. We believe that the existing SSA formulae have serious weaknesses (see paragraphs 3.15 – 3.24). We believe that it is possible to devise new grant formulae which avoid some of these weaknesses. But we are clear that any formula-based system has limitations. Accordingly, we are not prepared to rely wholly on formulae to distribute general grant.

3.11 Importantly, total reliance on grant formulae cannot take account of the circumstances or aspirations of individual authorities or offer any positive incentives to improve performance. These are unavoidable limitations of any formula-based grant distribution system. They are the main reason why it does not make sense to rely on formulae alone to distribute grant. A general grant system ought to encourage local authorities to become more efficient.

3.12 As proposed in the green paper, we intend to move to a structure in which there are three categories of revenue grant. The box below shows how the grants relate:

Ring-fenced grant	General grant	
Can only be used for the specified purposes	Has no conditions on how it is spent	
	Targeted grants	**Formula grant**
	Paid according to a different mechanism to formula grant; may have conditions on eligibility to receive the grant	Paid to all authorities under the grant formulae and the rules on floors and ceilings

3.13   We do not propose to take local authorities' own corporate plans into account in the grant distribution decision during this Parliament (see paragraphs 3.25 – 3.27). We believe that some of the objections to this approach were overstated or misconceived. However we have concluded that the level of central government judgements over local budgets is incompatible with our vision of empowered local government rather than local administration.

3.14   As noted in paragraph 1.20, reform of the revenue grant distribution system is an urgent priority for this Parliament but we must ensure that there is adequate time for preparation and consultation. We therefore announced in July our intention to extend the existing three-year formula freeze to cover 2002-03 and we will introduce new grant formulae in the 2003-04 settlement.

The problems with SSA

3.15   In devising a new grant system, we need to be clear what is wrong with the existing one. There are a number of specific problems with individual SSA formulae. In the Government's view, there are also more fundamental problems.

3.16   First, SSA has been presented as a measure of 'spending need'. This is highly misleading. The Government does not claim to know how much an individual authority should spend on a particular service. The reality is that SSA is merely a means of distributing Government grant, which is then topped up by local authorities from council tax. In their spending decisions, both central and local government are taking a view on what is affordable, as well as assessing cost pressures. In designing the new grant system, we shall seek to make the status of the grant formulae clearer.

3.17   Second, formulae driven entirely by annual changes in data will produce unpredictable annual variations in grant. For example, some authorities have experienced unexpectedly large changes to the estimates of their total populations or numbers of benefit claimants. Relatively small movements in interest rates have produced changes in entitlement under the capital finance SSA which have taken authorities by surprise. This leads to regular disputes about the data used.

3.18   It is, of course, important that where the formulae need data, this should be the best available data, independently produced and of general application to local authorities. But how the data are used is also important. Part of the solution is to make more use of data trends in the formulae, rather than a single year's figures. But the main way of dealing with the volatility produced by data and formula changes is via the introduction of floors and ceilings.

3.19   Third, the SSA formulae are not readily intelligible to the public or even to councillors and other key stakeholders. Some formulae have become too complex, because they are trying to achieve a spurious degree of precision or contain elements which do not obviously relate to the relative costs of providing services to most people. A key aim in the design of new grant formulae will be to make them as intelligible as possible.

3.20   Fourth, across the whole range of their activities, local authorities face a 'cost of being in business' as well as a 'cost of doing business'. There is a minimum, unavoidable cost involved in being a local authority – running elections, supporting councillors, controlling finances, undertaking best value reviews, etc. There is also a minimum, unavoidable cost of being a planning authority or education authority, of running a trading standards department or a library service, regardless of the size of the community served. This is not recognised by the current system.

3.21 Last but not least, the formulae rely heavily on the statistical technique of regression analysis against expenditure at the level of an individual local authority. This has the effect of replicating past patterns of spend, rather than looking at the spending pressures which authorities face today. This issue is a particularly important one. It is worth spelling out the arguments here more fully, because they underlie many of the criticisms of the fairness of the SSA system.

3.22 As the green paper noted, expenditure on services can vary between authorities for three very different reasons:

- all authorities have to take a political decision on the right balance between taxation and expenditure;

- some authorities are more efficient than others;

- there are factors beyond the control of any individual authority, such as regional variations in pay levels, the fact that services such as refuse collection cost more to provide in sparsely populated areas, or the fact that people in deprived areas of the country need more help from a variety of local authority services.

SSA seeks to identify this last group of factors. It assumes that, if there is a strong correlation between the amount that different local authorities spend on a service and a given variable, this suggests that the variable has a real impact on the cost of providing the service. In effect, it assumes that differences in authorities' political approaches and differences in their efficiency are distributed randomly and can be ignored as 'noise in the system'. Unfortunately,

this assumption is highly suspect. In 1991, there were many inner city authorities whose high spending levels were attributable to conscious political choice, rather than to the high cost of providing services, and there were a few such authorities with very low levels of efficiency. When regression analysis finds a correlation between (say) population density and the level of spend on a service, it is picking up these factors, as well as external factors beyond authorities' control.

3.23 Even if it were possible to isolate external factors which determined the cost of services in 1991 (which we doubt), there is no reason to suppose that their influence is the same in 2001 or will be the same in 2011. All of the services covered by the grant formulae are evolving. There is a much greater emphasis on prevention in today's fire service than there was 10 years ago. In the care of elderly people, there is a greater emphasis on helping them to live at home. Contracting-out has changed the way services are procured and IT has changed the way they are delivered.

3.24 The Government concludes that:

- There is no reason why we should not continue to use formulae to distribute the great majority of general grant between authorities.

- We need to look to amend the formulae to make them fairer and more intelligible.

- We also need to recognise that formulae have their limitations. They are a means of distributing grant, not an infallible guide to how much local authorities should spend. They are based on imperfect data, which provide a snapshot picture of cost pressures. They cannot take account of all the local circumstances of 432 different authorities.

- We cannot rely on formulae alone. They must be supplemented by other mechanisms.

Taking authorities' own plans into account

3.25 One of the key choices we had to make in the light of the green paper responses was what other mechanism should supplement grant formulae. Specifically, should the grant decision take account of local authorities' own plans. Amongst local authority respondents to the green paper, opponents of the use of plans outnumbered supporters by a margin of about 7:1. This fact carried weight with us, because we believe that the grant system needs to be 'owned' by both central and local government. So did the fact that it would probably take two or three years to introduce a plan-based approach, whereas it is our assessment that the grant system needs more urgent reform than that.

3.26 Production of good forward plans is important for all local authorities (see chapter 10) not an unwarranted additional burden on authorities. We made it clear in the green paper that the Government would not require any information in the plans submitted to it, which would not be needed to produce the authority's own plan. Nor do we accept that a plan-based approach would place an unmanageable burden on Government. Lastly, we do not accept that the appraisal of plans would involve second-guessing of authorities' council tax proposals or national priorities being given precedence over local ones. Both concerns rest on the mistaken view that the grant decision involves Ministers approving or disapproving individual proposals in the plan, rather than using it as the basis for a judgement on the overall amount of general grant to be paid to an authority.

3.27 The genuinely difficult aspect of a grant system which takes account of local authorities' own plans is that it involves Ministers taking a judgement on the spending pressures faced by different authorities and on the merits of each authority's spending plans. This level of central government judgement over local budgets is incompatible with our vision of local government, rather than local administration. We have therefore decided against plan-based grant decisions.

Targeted grant and local public service agreements

3.28 Instead of supplementing formulae by taking account of authorities' own plans, we shall adopt the alternative approach set out in the green paper – using targeted grant and local PSAs.

TARGETED GRANT

3.29 The green paper proposed to move beyond the traditional division between ring-fenced and general grant by introducing grant which is targeted but not ring-fenced. The box at paragraph 3.12 above shows the relationship between ring-fenced grant, targeted grant and formula grant. Targeted grant may be paid only to selected authorities, rather than to all authorities. It will be a named grant intended for a specific purpose. It can have conditions attached requiring stated outcomes and/or targets to be achieved.

3.30 The neighbourhood renewal fund (NRF) provides targeted grant. It is payable only to authorities which meet the deprivation criteria set out by Government. It also has conditions attached to it, such as the requirement to put in place a local strategic partnership, with whom the neighbourhood renewal strategy will be agreed. But NRF grant is not ring-fenced for any specific local authority service. It can be spent in whatever way the authority, together with the local strategic partnership, judges best to raise service standards in the most deprived neighbourhoods.

3.31   The performance reward grant which will be paid to authorities who meet the stretch targets in local PSAs is also targeted grant. There are conditions to be satisfied in order to get the grant, but no restrictions on how it is spent.

LOCAL PUBLIC SERVICE AGREEMENTS

3.32   We announced in the spending review white paper in July 2000 that we would extend the public service agreement approach to local authorities. We have tested the process by negotiating individual local PSAs with 20 pilot authorities, and over the next two years will roll out the programme to all counties, unitary authorities, metropolitan districts and London boroughs who wish to enter into a local PSA with Government. The key elements of the pilot scheme have been retained, and there are incentives to encourage districts and counties to work together on joint agreements. Rather than continuing to rely on the special grant power in the 1988 Act, we intend to seek a specific power to make local PSA grants.

3.33   The key features of local PSAs are:

- Local authorities identify around 12 specific targets where they believe that they can deliver more demanding service improvements over the next three years than currently expected. The majority of these targets relate to the national priority objectives which the Government set for itself in the 2000 spending review. Local PSAs also include local targets that relate to local priorities, often identified in best value consultation.

- Authorities also identify obstacles to delivering the targets which Government may be able to remove. They propose freedoms and flexibilities which they believe will make it more likely that they can achieve their more stretching targets.

- The achievement of the local PSA targets secures a financial reward, in the form of performance reward grant. An authority which meets all 12 targets will receive performance reward grant equivalent to 2½ per cent of one year's net budget requirement.

- The Government provides an average of around £1 million of 'pump-priming' grant to help an authority get new initiatives off the ground. This can be supplemented by access to unsupported credit approvals.

3.34   Local PSAs are agreed between central government and individual authorities. The Government has to satisfy itself that the targets are sufficiently demanding, focussed on outcomes and measurable. The local authority has to be satisfied that the targets address the needs of their area, and that the combination of performance incentives and agreed freedoms and flexibilities which the Government is able to give them offers sufficient scope to meet their stretching targets.

3.35   We shall not know what difference local PSAs have made to local services until we see how many of the demanding targets are met. Both local and central government want the targets to be met in full: the targets are intended to be challenging and realistic. However, it is already clear from the pilot agreements that local PSAs have a potentially important role to play in helping to deliver priority services. They plug a gap in the local government finance system and best value by creating a link between funding and performance, in a way that does not take anything away from people who live in areas served by poorly performing authorities. The requirement that a majority of the targets must relate to national priorities provides an alternative to ring-fencing as a means by which Ministers can promote the objectives which matter most to them – although authorities are free to spend their reward grant as they choose. They provide an opportunity for negotiation with central government, in which local authorities can identify their priorities. They have clarified both sides' understanding of where the obstacles to service improvement really lie – in many cases, the obstacles were over-estimated by the local authority or under-estimated by the Government department. In addition to the flexibilities and freedoms already agreed, the local PSAs identify a number of issues on which the Government is committed to further dialogue. We believe that local PSAs are a potentially powerful engine for change within local authorities and within Whitehall. This is particularly true on the finance side. Local PSA negotiations have identified ring-fencing of grants, plan-production requirements, rules on recovery of past grants and the treatment of revenue from fines as obstacles to service improvements.

3.36   The first local PSAs run until March 2004. Chapter 3 of part I sets out our plans for the future development of local PSAs. We intend to build on the good reception which local PSAs have received from both local and central government and continue the programme, focussing as now on rewarding improvements in performance. We will retain the main features of the present scheme, ensuring that agreements contain stretching targets addressing priority areas identified by the Government as well as local priorities. We will continue to welcome proposals for freedoms and

flexibilities which will help authorities to meet their targets, and will be prepared to agree more ambitious freedoms for authorities which the new performance assessment system recognises as good performers. We will also continue to encourage councils to work together with local partners, including districts, in developing their local PSA and delivering better outcomes.

How the formula grant will be allocated

3.37   We are committed to introducing new grant formulae, replacing SSA, from 1 April 2003. We shall announce in due course the principles we are applying in conducting this formula grant review.

3.38   It is not possible to predict the impact of new grant formulae at this stage. However, past experience shows that, even where formula changes have a modest impact at the national level (in terms of moving grant between regions or between classes of authority), they can still have a big impact on individual authorities. To prevent these formula or data changes having a disruptive effect on services or council tax bills, we shall continue to operate floors and ceilings where it is appropriate to do so.

CHAPTER 4
The way forward on capital investment

The starting point

4.1   For over a century local authorities have required Government permission to borrow. Since 1990 that permission has come in the form of a 'credit approval'. The Government issues credit approvals by sending authorities letters stating the amounts and kinds of capital investment they may lawfully fund from borrowing (and other sorts of credit). There are two types of credit approval. Basic credit approvals (BCAs) can be used to support any form of capital investment. Supplementary credit approvals (SCAs) are provided to support investment in specified services or for specified purposes. The distinction between BCAs and SCAs is similar to the distinction between general and ring-fenced grant.

4.2   Credit approvals have had three main effects. They have provided local people with protection against their local authority running up excessive debts, leading to council tax increases or cuts in services. They have made it easier for the Government to manage public finances at the national level. But they have also shifted decision-making responsibility from local to central government.

What the green paper said

4.3   The green paper said that the present capital control system blurs accountability, limits local financial freedom and has become an obstacle to effective capital investment. It proposed the abolition of the system of credit approvals. In its place, the green paper suggested that there should be a local prudential regime, under which individual authorities would determine for themselves how much it would be sensible for them to borrow. The green paper proposed transitional arrangements to guard against an unmanageable upsurge in local

government borrowing when Government control is removed. It also proposed reserve powers to deal with authorities which did not exercise the new freedom responsibly.

4.4   The green paper canvassed options for Government support for local authority capital investment. We could continue to lend local authorities money to fund the investment and pay them revenue grant to service the loan. Or we could move to the payment of capital grant. Whichever approach was adopted, the allocation of Government support would build on the single capital pot. We would also ensure that there was funding available to promote public private partnerships.

What you said

4.5   The proposal to abolish credit approvals received almost universal support. On balance, local authorities, businesses and other respondents all felt that it was right to give councils greater freedom and responsibility to decide for themselves how much they could prudently afford to borrow. Respondents believed that this was a valuable freedom.

4.6   Business respondents were concerned that the combination of increased Government support for capital investment and greater freedom to borrow might result in local authorities carrying out services in-house and funding capital investment themselves, even though better value for money could be secured by involving the private sector.

The Government's proposals

4.7   The Government will abolish credit approvals, and replace them with a new local prudential regime. There will be a statutory requirement for each local authority to set prudential limits for its borrowing (paragraphs 4.13 – 4.17), and stick to them. Local authorities will be expected to consult on their investment and borrowing plans (paragraph 4.20). Failure to set, and stick to, prudential limits could trigger the use of Government reserve powers to set a ceiling on the growth of an authority's borrowings (paragraph 4.23).

4.8   Government support for local authority capital investment will continue. Government will continue to consider options on the form that this support should take – whether revenue, capital or a mix of the two (paragraphs 4.25 – 4.27). The Government will continue to provide special grant to support private finance deals (paragraphs 4.33 – 4.36). The main benefits of the new system are summarised in the text box below.

Benefits of the new system

The main benefits of the new prudential system are as follows

- Authorities will be free to borrow for investment without Government consent, provided they can afford to service the debt

- That means more spending on locally important projects – e.g. promoting better quality of life

- Authorities will be more accountable and responsible

- Local people will have a greater say in decisions

- Authorities' spending will be less tied in to rigid annual bidding rounds

- The system will be simpler to operate and easier for officers, councillors and the public to understand

- The new freedoms will be balanced by sensible safeguards

4.9   Subject to the outcome of the separate consultation exercise now under way, we shall also reform the investments framework to bring it up-to-date and to give local authorities a useful degree of extra freedom on how they invest their temporarily surplus funds. We shall still strongly encourage the use of investments which are as safe as possible and which allow authorities easy access to their money when it is needed for expenditure.

Replacing credit approvals

4.10   The Government will legislate to abolish credit approvals. Local authorities will no longer require Government permission to borrow.

4.11   As chapter 1 makes clear, one of the aims of this paper's proposals is to give local authorities real financial freedom and responsibility. The abolition of credit approvals is a prime example of the new freedoms we are granting. But with this freedom comes a major new responsibility. Authorities will need to take on themselves the judgement of how much capital spending they can afford to finance from borrowing and other forms of credit. If they get the judgement wrong, they and local people will have to live with the consequences for many years. Excess levels of council tax can be corrected relatively easily and quickly, and voters can express their views by elections and referendums. But if an authority embarks on an ill-conceived or over-ambitious capital investment programme, it can take 15-20 years for the finances of the authority to recover. Voters can still register their disapproval in local elections, but the damage will have been done.

4.12   As noted in chapter 10, the Government will have power to help authorities which get into financial difficulties, but that help will be available only in the most exceptional cases. Where direct government support is required to deal with problems of an authority's own making, assistance is likely to be accompanied by the use of other powers of intervention and control. It is therefore essential that the new freedom is used wisely. The main means of ensuring this will be the introduction of the local prudential regime, backed up by appropriate public consultation. However, the Government will also take reserve powers.

THE LOCAL PRUDENTIAL REGIME

4.13 The local prudential regime is about self-regulation. It will require individual authorities to decide how much they can prudently borrow. They must set limits on the total amount of debt that they can take on. Having set these limits, the authority will be required to adhere to them. They will not be permitted to undertake new borrowings that would take them above their limits. They will be permitted to increase their ceiling for affordable debt in-year only if the new figure is still within prudential limits (for example, if it becomes evident during the year that estimates of revenue income can properly be adjusted upwards). We shall also ensure that local government officers (particularly, the S151 officer) and district auditors have the powers they need to ensure that the legal requirements are complied with. The new system, like the present one, will also apply when authorities obtain assets on long-term credit (such as leasing and hire purchase); authorities using such credit will have to decide whether it is affordable, just as if they were borrowing to buy the assets outright.

4.14 The locally set limit on an authority's borrowing will take account of all sources of estimated future revenue income and the potential calls on the use of that revenue. The amount of revenue income not required for other spending purposes will be potentially available to service the authority's debts and thus offers the best measure of the affordability of new borrowing. Local authority revenues have grown over time, as Government grant and council tax yields have increased in real terms. Council tax revenue is within the authority's own control, and the introduction of floors and ceilings on formula grant will protect authorities from the sort of annual fluctuations in grant that used to be a feature of SSA. This means that an authority can estimate for a number of years ahead the amount of revenue available to support debt after other essential commitments have been met.

4.15 It is not prudent for authorities to borrow against the security of their capital assets, since the potential seizure of property by creditors would pose an unacceptable threat to the delivery of services. In any case, the main lender to local authorities – the Public Works Loan Board – never requires such security. We shall therefore not remove the long-standing prohibition on the mortgaging of local authority property. Nor shall we allow authorities to 'securitise'– i.e. sell future streams of revenue income, such as rents, in return for immediate one-off payments. The prudential system should achieve all the financial flexibility that is needed and in a much safer way.

4.16 The calculation of the affordability of borrowing will need to be underpinned by unambiguous definitions of debt and revenue, which are applied uniformly by all authorities. CIPFA, in liaison with central and local government, is developing appropriate definitions and will publish them in a code with which all local authorities will be required to comply under the new legislation. The code will also specify other factors which authorities need to take into account, e.g. the level of reserves and outstanding debt. It will also describe the process to be followed in setting and monitoring prudential limits. The code cannot be finalised and issued until primary legislation on the prudential system is enacted. However, a first draft will be issued for consultation shortly.

4.17 Although it is important to get the 'machinery' of the local prudential regime right, the key to success is that authorities' members take the responsibility for setting the borrowing limit seriously. They will have to answer to voters if the prudential borrowing limit is set too high, leading to the sort of long-term problems described in paragraph 4.11. The CIPFA code can help them, by giving guidance and by ensuring that they get clear and professionally robust advice from officers. However, the Government, CIPFA and the authority's officers cannot do councillors' jobs for them. It is an essential feature of a local prudential regime that members set the borrowing limit.

INVESTMENT DECISIONS AND THE BUDGET PROCESS

4.18 Given the importance of revenue considerations in determining the affordability of borrowing, the Government will encourage authorities to adopt a coherent budgeting process which combines decisions on capital investment with the setting of the revenue budget and council tax levels. Such a process will feed into the production of the council tax leaflet, a capital strategy document and the best value performance plan. Authorities will need to look further ahead than one year in setting prudential limits for borrowing and, for this reason, the CIPFA code underpinning the new prudential system will introduce a requirement that authorities prepare three-year revenue budget forecasts.

4.19 Authorities are required to produce corporate capital strategies, setting out their intentions and approach on capital investment, as part of the single capital pot initiative. These strategies should cover all the functions for which they are responsible, and show how cross-cutting issues such as exclusion or sustainable development are being tackled. Strategies

should set out the corporate aims and principles that will underpin the production of the authorities' detailed capital programmes, and should address both national and local policy objectives. It is important that they also reflect and promote joint working with other partners in the public, private and voluntary sectors. With the introduction of prudential borrowing, capital strategies will include the suite of forward-looking prudential indicators (including the prudential limits and ratios) which support the Council's decision on the level of self-financed borrowing.

PUBLIC CONSULTATION

4.20 It is obviously important that local authorities undertake appropriate public consultation on their capital investment plans. If they wish to do so, local people should have the opportunity to have their say on the long-term commitments which their council intends to enter into on their behalf. They should have information on the likely impact of new borrowings on their council tax bills. They should also have access to a proper risk-assessment, based on the work which officers will have done for members, so that they can understand the consequences of cost overruns or revenue shortfalls. Capital strategies should be written primarily as a means of consulting and communicating with local people, businesses and partners. Set alongside the best value performance plans, they will give local people a comprehensive picture of the council's intentions. In some circumstances, an authority contemplating a particularly large or unusual investment might want to conduct some separate form of consultation. It would not be sensible to legislate on how the public are consulted in particular circumstances. But we shall seek evidence that appropriate consultation is taking place.

The new legislative framework for capital

The *legislative structure* of the new system will be as follows:

- **Primary legislation.** The measures will be kept as short and simple as possible. There will be broad powers for local authorities to finance their capital expenditure; and powers for the Government to regulate borrowing and other financing methods.

- **Regulations.** Any necessary detail will be relegated to the secondary legislation, including, for example, definitions of such concepts as credit and capital receipts. But a major function of the regulations will be to identify the various codes with which authorities will have to comply.

- **Codes of Practice.** We will be able to require compliance with any published codes, for example, of accountancy and treasury management. In particular, of course, these will include the prudential code specially developed by CIPFA. The Government will also be able to issue its own codes, for example, requiring authorities to make proper provision for debt repayment and for depreciation. The advantage of codes is that they enable complex financial concepts to be treated in a more flexible and intelligible way than is possible in legislation. At the same time they may be given the binding force of legislation.

Within that legislative structure, the key *control mechanisms* will be:

- **The prudential limits.** In accordance with the CIPFA prudential code, authorities will need to assess the affordability of financing options which depend upon borrowing (or credit). They will estimate the reliability and value of their various sources of revenue income over the next three years (with a broader look beyond). Against this will be offset potential calls on income, taking account of both commitments and contingencies (also making allowance for the inherent limitations of this estimating process). That will identify the amount of new long-term borrowing, if any, which can prudently be supported from the remaining income. Authorities will have power to borrow up to that amount without Government consent. Authorities will however in addition need to keep under review the ratio of their loan charges to revenue income. Significant increases in that ratio would have to be reported to the Council and would trigger a reconsideration of the basic affordability assessment.

- **Other prudential indicators.** The prudential code will specify other indicators which will serve as monitoring devices and checks upon the affordability calculation, such as the level of outstanding debt.

- **The national borrowing limit.** This would be the Government's means of overriding the prudential limit, if the latter seemed likely to allow a level of public expenditure which the national economy could not sustain. The limit would be set in regulations. It would allow authorities to undertake self-financed borrowing up to a specified maximum. This might be expressed as an annual cash amount or as a specified percentage increase in borrowing compared with the previous year. The legislation would however permit different formulae to be applied to different descriptions of authorities. Authorities could also transfer unwanted borrowing capacity to another authority, subject to the borrowings remaining within both local and national limits.

- **The individual borrowing limit.** This would work just like the national borrowing limit, but would apply to an individual authority, because it would only be applied on an exceptional basis. It would be imposed by a direction rather than regulations. Its imposition might be considered, for example, where an authority failed to set local prudential limits in accordance with the CIPFA Code or breached such limits, or showed in other ways that it could not cope with the freedoms.

GOVERNMENT RESERVE POWERS

4.21   The Government will take a reserve power to set a limit on the rate at which local authorities can increase their borrowings. This reserve power will serve two purposes:

- In the transitional period after the abolition of credit approvals, it could be used if necessary to ensure that there is not a short-term 'surge' in borrowing which would be unmanageable for the national economy. In the longer term, it could also be used if macro-economic conditions ever necessitated extra safeguards to keep public expenditure to levels that were nationally affordable.

- The same power will be used to deal with any individual authorities which fail to set a prudential limit or which breaches the limit.

4.22   In its regular spending reviews, the Government will decide how far local authority debt could be allowed to rise without risk to the national economy. It is expected that authorities' self-financed borrowing under the new prudential framework could normally be accommodated within that ceiling. However, if that level ever seemed likely to be exceeded, the reserve power could be used to set a formal upper limit. If the control were used at a national level, either during the transitional period or later, it would allow authorities to undertake borrowing financed from their own resources up to a specified maximum. The Government would prefer not to impose any national limit at the start of the new system, since it would represent a central control similar in principle to credit approvals. The decision on whether it will be necessary will depend upon estimates of the potential increase in borrowing and its effect on the economy which can only be made closer to the start of the new system. It is also not possible at this stage to say, if such a transitional limit were imposed, how long it would last; but it would be lifted as soon as we considered it safe to do so.

4.23   The borrowing freedoms under the new system will be available to all authorities (subject to any national limit) and will not be a reward for good performance. But if an individual authority abuses the new freedom, we shall be able to use the reserve power to set a limit on that authority's self-financed borrowing. As under the present system, scrutiny by the chief finance officer and external auditor will provide important safeguards against such abuse. The imposition of an individual limit would be an exceptional measure, triggered by serious failures to comply with the prudential code. In an extreme case, an authority could have such a limit imposed from the start of the new system, if there was strong evidence of serious financial failings.

Government support for capital investment

4.24   The Government has significantly increased its support for local authority capital investment. In 1997-98, central government support for local authority capital expenditure was £4 billion; it will increase to over £11 billion in 2003-04. The Government's policy on support for investment will not be affected by the abolition of credit approvals. The additional investment which local authorities will be able to undertake using the new borrowing freedom is intended to supplement Government supported investment, not replace it. Nor do we intend to increase support that is ring-fenced for specific purposes at the expense of support that is available to support any capital investment. The Government will continue to work towards fulfilling the commitment made in 1998 that the bulk of capital support should be provided in flexible, cross-service resources through the single capital pot (see 4.30 below).

THE FORM OF GOVERNMENT SUPPORT

4.25   In the green paper, the Government outlined two options for delivering support for capital investment: ongoing revenue support (RSG, as now) or a move to 100 per cent capital grants. The capital grants option would mean that Government support for local authority

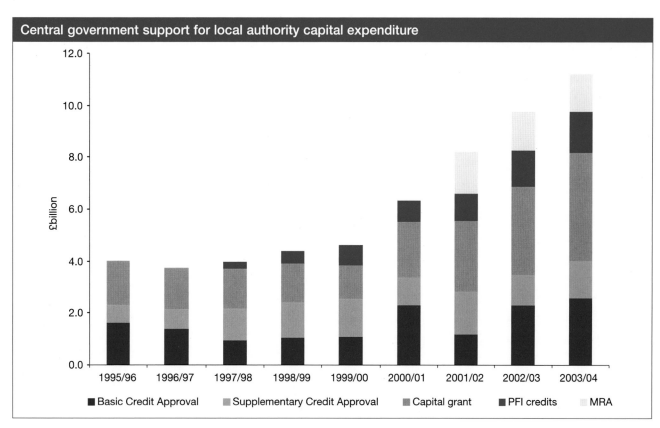

Central government support for local authority capital expenditure

£billion

■ Basic Credit Approval   ■ Supplementary Credit Approval   ■ Capital grant   ■ PFI credits   MRA

capital investment would take the form of up-front capital grant. This would provide for the major element of capital programmes and would mean the end of Government-supported borrowing. Authorities would still be able to borrow under the prudential system – but this would be unsupported by Government grant and the debt would have to be serviced by authorities themselves out of their revenue resources. If support continued to be provided through RSG, both supported and unsupported borrowing would be covered by the prudential system, with the RSG on the supported element being available to count towards local authority income in the affordability assessment. Under either option, RSG support for historic debt would continue.

4.26 Responses to the green paper showed a high level of interest in making increased use of capital grants, so long as this did not result in an increase in specific grants or bid-based allocation mechanisms. However, a number of respondents were also keen to ensure that Government support retained flexibility to deal with different approaches to procurement. Some responses also highlighted the desirability of moving towards a system which would better reflect true depreciation costs, an objective which the Government shares, although there would be issues of affordability to be addressed in such a move.

4.27 Decisions on the form of future Government support can be pursued separately from the work to develop and introduce the prudential system. The prudential system is capable of working equally effectively with revenue support, capital grants or a combination of the two. In the light of the green paper responses, the Government consider that it is worth taking more time to explore all the options for government support further, in consultation with local government, given the breadth of the issues, their relevance to developments in central/local relations highlighted in part one, and their links to issues such as the development of better asset management systems and the forthcoming introduction of Whole of Government Accounts.

HOW CAPITAL SUPPORT WILL BE ALLOCATED

4.28   Although credit approvals will no longer exist, the Government will continue to provide a mixture of general and ring-fenced support for capital investment. The single capital pot will continue as the vehicle for allocating general, cross-service capital support.

4.29   The first allocations through the single capital pot will be made for the 2002-03 financial year. £2.3 billion will be allocated, 95 per cent on a largely needs-based formula and 5 per cent on a discretionary basis. The 5 per cent will be allocated by taking into account authorities' performance in provision of the services funded through the pot (transport, housing, education and social services) as well as their approach to corporate capital planning and asset management.

4.30   For the first year of the single capital pot, the amount distributed represents just under half of the total that could potentially be directed through the pot. The Government will act to increase this share to fulfil its commitment to provide the bulk of local authority support in this way. The Government will use the performance assessment framework to identify those local authorities that have demonstrated their capacity to deliver on national priorities. For these authorities, the proportion of capital provided through the pot (and thus not ring-fenced) will be substantially increased. This will apply to those councils assessed as high performing or striving under the performance

assessment framework, though it will be subject to the judgement of the sponsoring government department as to whether the broader assessment is reflected in performance in the relevant service area. Selective ring-fencing, on either a service by service basis or for a whole authority, will remain for those authorities whose performance and ability to deliver is assessed as coasting or poor.

4.31   Local authorities have provided regional Government Offices with their corporate capital strategies and corporate asset management plans for assessment as part of the discretionary single pot element. A broader initiative to ease the plans burden on local authorities is set out in part one. In line with this, the requirement to submit these documents to Government will be relaxed for those authorities whose submissions in 2002 are assessed as 'good'. Authorities will continue to produce capital strategies as a means of consulting and informing stakeholders and to reassure both their council taxpayers and external auditor that an appropriate affordability assessment underpins their planned level of self-financed borrowing (see 4.13 above). However, these corporate documents will no longer be assessed by Government. For corporate asset management plans, the intention was always that these would be submitted only until sufficient improvement had been made in local authority asset management. As local authorities pass the threshold, Government will require only basic asset management data for corporate plans, comprising property performance indicators and information on asset numbers, values and condition. However, the relaxation in plan requirements does not mean that Government will not continue to encourage and expect improved asset management in local authorities. Authorities' capital planning and asset management, as demonstrated in capital strategies and property performance indicators, will form a key area for scrutiny as part of the performance assessment framework. Education AMPs have been developed and introduced in advance of the corporate AMPs and serve significantly wider purposes. They directly inform allocations of capital support to councils, as well as providing a basis for local improvement through the benchmarking of data and performance. They are still in the process of development, for instance to support better management of capacity and options appraisal. These and other differences mean that the requirement to submit Education AMPs, including information on priorities and processes, will continue, although the Department for Education and Skills will look to reduce the information needed for high performing councils, and will publish guidance on improving the joining-up of Education AMPs with councils' wider corporate documents.

4.32 Under the existing system, an authority's entitlement to credit approvals takes into account the receipts that it generates from the sale of assets through the receipts taken into account (RTIA) adjustment. This is a form of 'resource equalisation', similar to the adjustment made on the revenue grant side to take account of variations in the amount of council tax that authorities can raise. However, the council tax adjustment is designed to avoid creating any perverse incentives – a council's grant entitlement is not affected by its success in collecting council tax. The current receipts adjustment creates an incentive for councils not to dispose of assets. It is a complex mechanism, of limited impact and it creates uncertainty in authorities' forward projections of capital support. There is no place for the RTIAs adjustment, or a successor to it, in the simpler, more transparent capital control system being introduced. In line with a wider white paper initiative to deregulate and reduce red tape, the Government will act to abolish it. Different considerations, however, apply in the case of

housing capital receipts where there is a need for a more flexible alternative to the present method of redistribution through the 'set aside' mechanism (see chapter 5).

Public-private partnerships

4.33 Giving authorities extra borrowing capacity might at first seem inconsistent with the exploration of PFI and other partnership approaches. In practice there is no conflict. The capital finance system itself should be neutral as to the form of procurement adopted and should ensure that authorities' purchasing strategies are based solely on considerations of best value.

4.34 However, we recognise that authorities may require encouragement and incentives to explore innovative alternatives to traditional procurement methods. Accordingly, for the past four years the Government has been allocating additional revenue grant to support schemes under the local government Private Finance Initiative, which is one partnership approach, now well-established. The operation of the PFI grant system will be considered in parallel with the overall review of local government finance. Authorities with approved PFI schemes can expect support to be maintained, regardless of the future shape of the revenue and capital finance systems. The Government has encouraged authorities to look at all forms of procurement by requiring a council's approach to PFI/PPP and its corporate policies on procurement to be set out in its capital strategy.

4.35 The Government will also continue to encourage authorities to explore the areas in which PFI can achieve best value. We are currently launching a new programme to support PFI schemes for improving public access to information and services. This will encourage authorities to bring together under one roof a range of facilities provided by various authorities and agencies. Such projects, including the popular 'one-stop shops', will make a valuable contribution to the improvement and rationalisation of capital assets in accordance with authorities' capital strategies and asset management plans. We are considering how to stimulate interest in other innovative partnership and procurement arrangements, taking full account of the investigation of partnership working initiated by our consultation paper *Working with others to achieve Best Value* (March 2001).

4.36   We are also considering how local authority owned companies should be treated. At the moment, transactions by a company under the effective control of a local authority are treated as if undertaken by the authority. Borrowing by the company therefore scores against the parent authority's capital resources. That broad effect is to be preserved but the present complex mechanism is likely to be replaced by an accounting based test, involving the notional consolidation of the balance sheets of the company and the authority. The definition of a controlled company is set out in Part V of the Local Government and Housing Act 1989 and we will also consider updating this in line with modern accounting practice. Companies operating fully commercially, without local authority subsidy or guarantees and with a good record of profitability, could be considered for exemption from the controls.

Options for borrowing and investing

4.37   Local authorities will continue to have access to the PWLB, if they so wish, on very much the same basis as at present, including for self-financed borrowing. They will also remain free to borrow from commercial banks and other financial institutions. In addition they will, as now, be able to borrow by issuing bonds and other money-market instruments. Authorities choosing to go to the private market have no difficulty in raising loans without having formal credit ratings and we shall continue to discourage authorities from incurring the unnecessary expense of obtaining ratings. As for very many years, money borrowed by an authority from whatever source will still be secured on *all* the revenues of the authority. That arrangement gives lenders a high degree of confidence in authorities' creditworthiness. We have no intention of allowing a loan to be secured on the revenues expected from a particular project, which would confer no benefit but would increase borrowing costs. Nor will we allow authorities to mortgage their property or 'securitise' revenue streams (see paragraph 4.15 above). Neither the PWLB nor commercial lenders will be expected to establish whether the authority's borrowing is within its prudential limits and will remain protected as now if an authority's borrowing should turn out to be unlawful.

4.38   In their responses to the green paper, some authorities raised the question of local authority's lending and cash-investment powers. The new legislation will give authorities an explicit power to invest. The system will still encourage authorities to focus on security when investing, but we are currently consulting authorities on the design of the overall framework for the management of their surplus funds. The present regime will be simplified and we are considering giving authorities access to new options which should offer even greater security than those in the present regulations and hopefully a better return. One important new form of investment will be made available in advance of the new legislation. Financial involvement by a local authority in a company in its area purely to promote the local economy will be exempt from the normal constraints on the investment of surplus funds. The new system will encourage authorities to take an integrated view of the processes of borrowing, investment and capital spending and generally to follow professional guidance on sound treasury management.

New investments options

The options on which we are consulting include:

- Scrapping the present complex regulations in favour of more flexible statutory codes of practice

- Allowing access to commercial money market funds (pooled investment vehicles based mainly on short-term loans to highly rated companies), the best of which offer good interest, easy withdrawals and high security

- Introducing a broadly similar deposit facility run by the Government itself where authorities could place funds through the Public Works Loan Board (PWLB)

- Allowing longer term investments offering better returns and the certainty of an interest rate fixed for more than the 12 months now permitted

The PWLB deposit facility could be introduced in advance of the new legislation, under existing powers; and we shall aim to do that as soon as possible, if the consultation indicates sufficient demand for it. Other changes can best be handled under the new capital finance system, when we can build practical guidelines and safeguards into statute-backed codes rather than intricate legislation.

The consultation ends on 1 February 2002.

CHAPTER 5
The way forward on housing finance

The new approach

5.1   We are adopting a radical new approach to funding council housing which is consistent with our general policy that high-performing authorities should be eligible for increased financial freedoms. The key elements of our new approach are:

- The housing revenue account (HRA) will be greatly simplified. Rent rebates will be removed from it, making it a straightforward landlord account.

- The HRA subsidy system will also be simplified. Subsidy will eventually be calculated on the basis of the rents that should actually be charged and realistic estimates of the costs authorities need to incur.

- Subject to prudential limits, councils will be free to borrow against the revenues in their HRA, apart from their Major Repairs Allowance (MRA).

- Councils that establish high-performing arms length management organisations (ALMOs) will, within limits set in the spending review, be free to retain the proceeds of their rent increases to the extent necessary to fund the borrowing required to enable them to upgrade their stock to the decent homes standard.

- The current housing 'set aside' arrangement will be replaced by a simpler housing capital receipts pooling system that will apply to all housing receipts, including those received by debt-free authorities.

The starting point

5.2   Our housing objective is to give everyone the opportunity of a decent home.

5.3   The challenges we face include:

- Bringing all social housing (both council housing and housing owned by Registered Social Landlords (RSLs)) up to a decent standard by 2010. At present we estimate that some 1.7 million social homes fall short of the decent homes standard.

- Tackling homelessness and the severe shortages of affordable housing in certain parts of the country.

- Addressing the problems caused by the lack of demand for housing in other parts of the country, including in extreme cases the abandonment of some neighbourhoods.

- Tackling disrepair in privately owned housing occupied by low income households. Of the 20 per cent poorest owner-occupiers, 1.6 million households (53 per cent) live in accommodation that does not meet the decent homes standard.

Local authorities have a key role to play in all of these areas, both as providers of services (particularly as landlords) and in ensuring that all interested parties work together to develop and implement solutions within an agreed strategy. The local government finance system needs to support them in this work, both by providing the necessary resources and by providing incentives to efficient delivery.

5.4   Money is often a key component of solutions to housing problems. In addition to funding from local authorities' own resources there are two main local authority funding regimes:

- Revenue support to council-owned housing is provided through the HRA subsidy system. This is currently some £400 million a year (excluding the support paid towards the cost of the rent rebates that councils are obliged to give those eligible for housing benefit).

- Capital support is provided through the housing investment programme (HIP). This is currently some £800 million a year. It is used to:

    – provide grants to RSLs for the construction of new social homes;

    – support improvements to privately owned homes occupied by low income households; and,

    – improve council-owned stock.

For many authorities that continue to be landlords their housing programmes are their largest single item in terms both of revenue and capital expenditure.

5.5   Our current housing finance systems are extremely complicated and poorly understood. We need simpler and more transparent arrangements that are more sharply focussed on addressing the pressing housing problems we face. In particular, open government demands that councillors and tenants, as well as housing professionals, should be able to understand how the available public resources are distributed and how spending priorities are determined at both national and local level.

Delivering decent council housing: the revenue subsidy system

5.6   Council housing has a bespoke revenue finance regime. Broadly speaking, every authority with 50 or more council dwellings is required to maintain a ring-fenced HRA within its general fund. This is because, uniquely amongst major local authority services, council housing is largely funded by rental income (including the central government subsidy towards the cost of rent rebates) and the Government believes that it would be wrong for council housing either to subsidise or be subsidised by the general council taxpayer.

5.7   The HRA system has been developing in parallel with the rest of local government finance. Following extensive consultations with local authorities, housing professionals and accounting bodies, we have introduced a new financial framework for local authority housing. All authorities owning stock are expected to prepare HRA business plans based on comprehensive housing needs assessments and stock surveys. They are also required to keep their HRA on a resource accounting basis, including making provision for depreciation, which the Government is supporting through the MRA.

5.8   We operate the HRA subsidy system to enable all councils to manage, maintain and improve their stock whilst charging affordable rents. We run the regime as a national system, taking surpluses from the richer authorities and using them, with additional central government funding, to subsidise the poorer authorities. Were we not to run the system on this redistributive basis we would either need to increase central government support substantially or poorer councils would need to increase rents very dramatically. Even those authorities that contribute to the subsidies received by other authorities are still receiving a 'hidden subsidy' as they are not required to make a return on the capital tied up in their stock (apart from servicing any debt that may be attributable to the stock).

5.9 The HRA subsidy system does two things:

- it calculates the surplus or deficit an authority ought to have by making assumptions about its costs and revenues. Those assumptions are, however, far out of step with reality: on average councils charge 16 per cent more rent than assumed and spend 25 per cent more on management and maintenance than assumed. Where there is an assumed deficit the authority receives a 'housing element subsidy' equal to that deficit. Where there is an assumed surplus, that amount is generally used by the Government to help meet the cost of subsidies to poorer authorities.

- The system also pays rent rebate subsidy to recompense local authorities for the rebates they are required to allow tenants who are eligible for housing benefit. This is payable up to a limit rent. Should an authority choose to set an average rent above this level it would be required to meet itself the cost of rebates above the limit rent.

5.10 In practice, rather than a council with a housing element surplus making a payment to the Government only to receive a larger amount back as rent rebate subsidy, the amount that would be due to be paid to the Government is netted off the rent rebate subsidy and the balance is paid to the authority. Where the housing element surplus exceeds the rent rebate subsidy payable to the authority, no payment is made in either direction, but the council must transfer the net surplus to its general fund. Whilst this netting-off arrangement might make no difference in financial terms, it makes it harder to understand what is going on.

5.11 Overall, the HRA system is not well understood and is very far from transparent. A number of measures to simplify the system have already been announced including:

- removing rent rebates and rent rebate subsidy from the HRA, thus making the HRA a true landlord account in which the costs and income can be plainly seen;

- introducing an explicit pooling arrangement for the surpluses generated by some authorities, with the proceeds from the pool being used to meet some of the cost of subsidising those authorities that cannot cover their costs from their income. This will do no more than make clear what already happens; and,

- those authorities that have a housing element surplus that exceeds their rent rebate subsidy entitlement will in future pay all of their surplus into the pool and not pay any into their general fund, thus stopping a leakage of funding from council housing.

5.12 Last December's housing policy statement, *The Way Forward for Housing*, announced that all social rents are to be set on the basis of a common formula reflecting the value of a property, its size and manual earnings in the area. This will remove the current large discrepancies between the rents charged for similar properties by different councils and RSLs, whilst ensuring that rents remain affordable and generally well below private sector levels. The discrepancies are not only grossly unfair to those who pay their own rent, but they also distort the social rented market. This means that in many cases tenants do not face rational choices between paying more for a better property or less for a less attractive property. It can, in particular, inhibit tenants from moving to a smaller property as they may not make a worthwhile saving in their rent. It also means that the market does not provide RSLs with clear signals about where additional social housing is needed and where it is not.

5.13 The HRA subsidy system needs to be adjusted to reflect rent restructuring. In particular, the rent that the system assumes councils charge needs to be adjusted so that it is equal to the rent set by the rent restructuring formula. Similarly, the rent up to which the Government will meet the cost of rent rebates – the limit rent – needs to be moved to the same figure. These changes will be made gradually over ten years, as will the changes to the rents actually charged. By the end of this transitional period, the subsidy system will be based on the actual rents that councils should be charging, not some figure that bears little relation to the real world. The net result will be a clearer, more transparent and fairer system.

5.14   One of the consequences of rent restructuring is that council rents will, on average, rise by a small amount a year for each of the next ten years, (although this increase will be smaller than it has been over the last ten years). Decisions have yet to be taken on what will happen to the proceeds of these rent increases. Options include:

- allowing local authorities to spend more on management and maintenance, should there be a need for this;

- allowing certain councils to retain more of their income to enable them to increase investment in order to achieve the decent home standard. This is discussed more fully in paragraph 5.21 below;

- using the resources for housing or other expenditure outside the HRA.

All of these options will be considered in the forthcoming spending review.

5.15   Concerns have been expressed that the effect of moving the assumptions made about rents up to the formula rent might be to reduce the aggregate level of resources available to local authorities. There is no intention that these technical changes should be used either to reduce or increase the aggregate level of resources available to councils nationally. Indeed, the starting assumption in the forthcoming spending review will be that these changes should be resource neutral overall. The review will take into account the projected real terms increase in rents in the local authority sector and then consider how the additional resources should be used.

Capital investment in council owned stock

5.16   Currently there are four options for capital investment in the existing council stock:

- Continued direct management of the stock using the resources provided through the MRA and whatever proportion of the authority's HIP/single capital pot allocation and other resources the authority chooses to devote to improving its own stock.

- Establishing an ALMO to discharge the authority's landlord responsibilities. Under this option the stock remains in local authority ownership and the tenants remain tenants of the authority. Additional resources are available if such a company is set up and achieves either a 2* or 3* rating from the Housing Inspectorate.

- Transfer of the stock to an RSL.

- The private finance initiative.

5.17   The removal of the current controls on local authority borrowing will apply to borrowing for HRA expenditure and will provide a useful degree of flexibility for councils that opt for either of the first two options.

5.18 As with the rest of the general fund, local authorities will be free to borrow to fund increased capital investment within the HRA as long as they have the resources to service the additional borrowing. Authorities may, for example, choose to use some of the resources they currently use to pay for capital expenditure direct from their HRA. This would enable councils to bring forward investment that they might otherwise have been able to afford only over a longer period. This might be particularly attractive for 'spend to save' investment that would reduce costs in later years. Councils will, of course, have to ensure that they do not pre-empt resources they will need to meet their maintenance and management liabilities and for renewal expenditure, including unforeseen contingencies. For this reason, authorities will not be permitted to borrow against their MRA.

5.19 Subject to legislation, we would aim to implement the new system by April 2004, or earlier if possible.

5.20 Borrowing funded by HRA revenues will only be available for investment in HRA assets. Similarly, HRA revenues should not be taken into account in determining prudential borrowing limits for non-HRA borrowing.

Additional investment by councils to deliver decent council housing

5.21 The Government recognises that significant additional investment will be needed in the stock that remains in local authority ownership over and above that which could be afforded using the MRA and the HIP allocations at the current levels. To ensure that the additional resources that are earmarked in the spending review for this purpose are used as

effectively as possible, the Government proposes that they should only be made available after councils have established a high performing ALMO. In future, once the new borrowing freedoms have been introduced, such ALMOs will be able to retain a significantly larger proportion of their revenues to enable them to afford the additional borrowing required to pay for the extra investment needed to ensure that all of their housing meets the decent homes standard by 2010. Such ALMOs will generally still be required to contribute to the redistributive pool that will collect surpluses from the richer authorities and use them to support poorer councils. However, their contribution to the pool will be reduced to allow them headroom they need to fund the necessary investment. The size of the reduction of the pool contribution will be assessed on the basis of the ALMO's draft Business Plans which will be presented when they apply to establish an ALMO.

5.22 There may be some ALMOs that are net recipients from the redistributive pool. Such companies would receive a larger housing element subsidy as well as retaining all of their revenues.

5.23 The additional housing element subsidy paid to some ALMOs and the reduced contributions to the redistributive pool paid by others will be funded from the proceeds of the rent increases necessary to achieve rent restructuring, not by reducing the net resources available to other housing authorities.

5.24 The precise details of the new system and the sums of money involved will be determined in the 2002 Spending Review.

Re-investing the proceeds of the disposal of HRA asset sales

5.25   The current capital finance regime requires councils to 'set aside' 75 per cent of the proceeds of the disposal of HRA assets (e.g. income from 'right to buy' sales) to offset debt. As a consequence of this the HRA subsidy paid to an authority with set aside receipts is reduced by an amount that equates to the annual cost of the debt service charges on the set aside receipt. This reduction in revenue support is taken into account when decisions are made about the level of resources that can be provided to support new investment by local authorities. The net effect of set aside is therefore to redistribute a proportion of the capital spending power of HRA receipts.

5.26   The Government believes that it is right that the proceeds of the disposal of council housing assets should be ploughed back into council housing as those assets were largely funded by central government. We therefore believe that a mechanism with a redistributive effect similar to set-aside should be retained in the new capital finance regime. Indeed, without it there would need to be a substantial increase in public expenditure to ensure that the necessary capital spending power was provided in the right place to deliver the local authority element of the decent homes PSA target. The Government also sees no reason why authorities that are currently debt-free should be exempt from the requirement to contribute a proportion of their HRA receipts to a redistributive pool.

5.27   The current set aside mechanism is unnecessarily complex. It will be replaced by a two-part regime which will have the effect of creating a pool of receipts that can be used to fund new capital investment wherever the need is greatest:

- for authorities with debt attributable to their HRA, HRA support for debt charges will be reduced to reflect the proportion of receipts which the authority is required to contribute to the redistributive pool; and,

- for authorities without HRA debt, a specified proportion of the HRA receipts will have to be paid into the pool.

Funding non-HRA housing investment

5.28   If we are to deliver a decent home for all a great deal needs to be done beyond bringing council housing up to the decent homes standard. In parts of the country there is a serious shortage of affordable homes; in others the lack of demand and the abandonment of neighbourhoods is a major problem. Throughout the country, parts of the private sector stock are in a poor condition. Local housing authorities have a vital strategic role in bringing all relevant parties together to develop sustainable solutions to whatever housing problems exist in their area and region. As part of this, the HIP provides resources for capital investment. These are used, along with authorities own resources, to provide renewal grants to low income owner occupiers and local authority social housing grants to enable RSLs to provide new social housing as well as funding investment in council housing.

5.29   At present 95 per cent of HIP allocations are formulaic and based largely on a range of indicators of housing need. The Department has just completed an annual review of various aspects of the formulae in consultation with local authorities, housing associations and others and some updating of the indices has been possible. However, it has proved impossible to reflect all of the dimensions of need that we would ideally have liked to incorporate in the indicators. This is partly due to the complexity of the problems we face and partly to the lack of suitable data at the district and sub-district level. More fundamentally, doubts have emerged as to whether it is possible to reflect with sufficient precision in a set of formulae the complex pattern of need for housing investment. Indeed, some have implicitly concluded that this is not possible and argued for new funds to be created to tackle specific problems in certain parts of the country. The Department therefore proposes to conduct a fundamental review of the current formulaic approach to allocating HIP resources. In the interim the recently announced revised needs indices will be used for at least the next two annual allocations.

5.30 The Government would welcome views on whether the best solution is to acknowledge the limitations of a formulaic approach and to move to a regime in which, say, within each region 70 per cent of HIP resources are allocated by formulae and the remaining 30 per cent is distributed on the basis of a qualitative assessment of need made by Government Offices reflecting strategic priorities identified in Regional Housing Statements and an assessment of local authority housing strategies. Allocations between regions would continue to be made on the basis of the formulaic approach. This would align the HIP process more closely to that adopted by the Housing Corporation for the Approved Development Programme.

CHAPTER 6
The way forward on council tax

The starting point

6.1   Property taxes have a long history. One of the main reasons for producing the Domesday Book was to establish how much land people owned and how much tax they could pay on it. Up until 1990, the tax on residential property took the form of a domestic rate. Each property had a rateable value, which was based on its notional rental value. In 1990, the domestic rate was replaced by the community charge (or 'poll tax'), which was a tax based on the number of adults occupying a house or flat, rather than the value of the property. The community charge was unpopular, and did not survive long. It was replaced in 1993 by the council tax.

6.2   Like the old domestic rate, the council tax is essentially a property tax. But there are four important differences:

- Valuations are based on capital value of the property, not on the rental value.

- For council tax valuation purposes, properties are allocated to one of eight fairly broad value bands – see the table below.

- As the table also shows, council tax bills do not increase in direct proportion to property values. A property at the top of band E is worth three times as much as a property at the top of band A, but pays only twice as much council tax.

- The full rate of council tax is paid on houses or flats occupied by two or more adults. Properties occupied by only one adult get a 25 per cent discount. Second homes and long term empty properties currently get a 50 per cent discount. Exemptions are set nationally to cover a range of circumstances such as a property being left empty because the sole resident leaves to receive or provide care.

Council tax bands

	Range of values (1991 prices)	Range of values (2001 prices)	Average council tax bill
Band A	Up to £40,000	Up to £70,000	£601
Band B	£40,001 – £52,000	£70,001 – £90,000	£701
Band C	£52,001 – £68,000	£90,001 – £120,000	£801
Band D	£68,001 – £88,000	£120,001 – £155,000	£901
Band E	£88,001 – £120,000	£155,001 – £210,000	£1,102
Band F	£120,001 – £160,000	£210,001 – £280,000	£1,302
Band G	£160,001 – £320,000	£280,001 – £560,000	£1,502
Band H	Over £320,000	Over £560,000	£1,803

The table shows the eight council tax bands, as defined in the legislation, which is based on 1991 property values. It also shows approximately what range of prices that would equate to at today's prices, according to the DTLR All-lenders mix-adjusted house price index, which assumes that value changes since 1991 are spread evenly across England and across bands. The last column shows the council tax bill for each band based on the national average council tax of £901 at Band D.

6.3   Local authorities, including police authorities, fire authorities and the Greater London Authority, are funded by the council tax. The different components are brought together in a single council tax bill for each household. In areas with both a district and a county council, council tax bills are issued by district councils. In London, they are issued by the boroughs and the City of London.

6.4   Although council taxes are set locally, the Government has reserve powers to 'cap' them. Under the previous administration, this took the form of 'crude and universal' capping, under which the Government announced in advance the maximum budget increase that it was prepared to permit all authorities. We have introduced more selective reserve powers, designed to protect local people from excessive increases, rather than to control council tax levels generally.

6.5   Separately, we introduced a council tax benefit subsidy limitation scheme to ensure that authorities making steep council tax increases contribute to the additional council tax benefit costs they impose on national taxpayers.

What the green paper said

6.6   The green paper noted that the council tax is working well as a local tax. It has been widely accepted by taxpayers and is generally well understood. The banding system makes tax bills predictable and stable. The green paper did not propose reforms to the structure of the council tax. Nor did it propose any changes to the recently introduced reserve capping powers.

6.7   The green paper did propose introducing a fixed council tax revaluation cycle. It also flagged up some of the problems with council tax benefit subsidy limitation – particularly the complexity of the scheme. It suggested that, in two-tier areas, it might improve accountability if

council tax bills were issued by county councils, which typically account for about 80 per cent of the expenditure covered by the bill.

What you said

6.8   There was strong support for a fixed cycle of council tax revaluation. Some respondents felt that the Government should undertake a council tax revaluation as soon as possible.

6.9   Many respondents raised questions about the fairness of the tax. They thought the council tax bands should be revised to make the council tax more 'progressive', so that council tax bills would rise more steeply in line with valuation bands. Some also thought that the council tax revaluation should be accompanied by the creation of additional council tax bands.

6.10   There was strong support for abolishing council tax benefit subsidy limitation. Respondents agreed that it was complex and not well understood.

6.11   There were mixed views on billing arrangements. Many respondents recognised that the current arrangements are potentially confusing. But the majority of district councils were very reluctant to see billing responsibility transferred to county councils.

The Government's proposals

6.12   The Government will legislate to require properties to be revalued for council tax purposes every ten years (see paras 6.17 – 6.19). Work on the first revaluation will commence in 2005 and be completed in time for the council tax bills issued in 2007. The revaluation should not lead to a change in the overall council tax yield. We shall devise a transitional relief scheme in which the gainers contribute towards the costs of the losers for a transitional period (paragraph 6.20).

6.13   Ahead of the revaluation we will listen to the views of taxpayers and local government about council tax bands and related matters. We shall legislate to make it clear that additional council tax valuation bands can be created without further primary legislation (paragraphs 6.21-6.26).

6.14   As part of our deregulatory agenda, we will abolish council tax benefit subsidy limitation and we will not use the reserve capping powers against high performing authorities (paragraphs 6.32-6.42).

6.15   We are consulting on giving local authorities greater discretion to set local policy on council tax discounts and exemptions. Although the existing framework of national discounts and exemptions will continue, local authorities will have the freedom to reduce or end the discount given for second homes or long-term empty homes, and will also be able to create further exemptions or discounts as they see fit, subject to meeting the costs locally. (paragraphs 6.43 – 6.61)

6.16   We shall not pursue the transfer of billing responsibility from district councils to county councils during this Parliament. Instead, we have reformed the billing regulations to make council tax increases more transparent to taxpayers (paragraphs 6.47 – 6.51). We will legislate to make combined fire authorities major precepting authorities (paragraphs 6.52 – 6.53).

Revaluation

6.17   Government fully recognises the importance of keeping property values up to date. This was not done under the domestic rates, which caused the tax to fall into disrepute and was one factor behind the introduction of the poll tax. However, for the reasons given in paragraph 1.22 we believe that it would be unacceptably disruptive to conduct a council tax revaluation in parallel with reform of the revenue grant system. Unlike when the previous administration introduced the council tax, we do not want to rush a revaluation. It is a major exercise and will benefit from time taken to plan and consult on detailed aspects such as proposals for a transitional relief scheme.

6.18   The green paper noted the need to integrate the council tax and business rate revaluation cycles. It would impose a significant burden on the Valuation Office Agency and others if a council tax and business rate revaluation had to be carried out in parallel. The green paper consulted on six, eight or ten-yearly revaluations of both taxes. However, it was clear from green paper responses that businesses were unwilling to see any significant reduction in the current frequency of business rate revaluations. And the Government is clear that a five-yearly council tax revaluation would be too frequent. It is not necessary for a council tax revaluation to be as frequent as the business rate revaluations, because council tax is based on broad valuation bands. And a council tax revaluation is expensive. We estimate that it would cost over £100 million to carry out a council tax revaluation, depending on the number of appeals against the new property values.

6.19   The Government will introduce legislation requiring domestic properties to be revalued for council tax purposes every ten years. The council tax and business rate revaluation cycles will be integrated. The council tax revaluation will follow two years after every second business rate revaluation. The new property values will be used for council tax bills in 2007.

6.20   Ahead of the revaluation, we shall consult on proposals for a transitional relief scheme, and seek from Parliament the necessary legislative powers. There is a clear case for phasing in the effects of these changes, particularly for the small proportion of properties moving up two or more bands. Ideally, this should be self-financing, in the same way as the transitional relief scheme for business ratepayers. The cost of phasing in the increased bills for the properties that increase their banding would be offset by also phasing in the reductions for those that move down. However, because the council tax is based on bands and because council tax levels are set by individual authorities, we shall need to devise a slightly different approach from the one proposed for business rates (see chapter 7).

Council tax revaluation

There are two important starting points:

- There should not be any change in the amount of council tax collected

- The average property value in England has increased considerably since 1991, when properties were last valued for council tax purposes.

So a revaluation will involve adjusting the council tax bands to reflect general movements in property values. Every home in England will be placed in a new band based on its value in 2005, with revised bills being issued in 2007.

If a property has risen in value by more than the national average, it would be likely to go up a band (or possibly more than one band). But every increase should be balanced out by other properties going down by one (or more) bands.

The fairness of the tax

6.21   Local authorities, academics and other experts have made two main criticisms about how the council tax works in some areas of the country.

6.22   First, it is not a 'progressive' tax in terms of the link between tax paid and property values. Some argue that the tax should be made more progressive through steeper ratios between bands. Another concern is that the bands are not fine grained enough to reflect differences in value at the top and bottom of the property market. In some areas band A covers very basic properties as well as more spacious properties with better facilities. Residents of mobile homes and other very low-value properties are particularly aggrieved, and have added to calls to split band A.

6.23   Second, this simple link between property value and tax paid ignores important variations in property values and ability to pay. There are many pensioners on low and fixed incomes in high value properties. The difference in house prices between London and the North-East is much greater than the difference between average incomes in the two regions. Many rural areas have house prices above the national average, because they are popular locations for second homes, whilst income levels are well below the national average. Many owner-occupiers whose homes are placed in higher valuation bands following a council tax revaluation would have seen substantial equity gains – but this is not true for council taxpayers who rent their homes. There has been no systematic gathering of evidence on the relationship between property values and incomes.

6.24   Despite these criticisms, the council tax does its present job – funding one quarter of local authority revenue spend – reasonably well. Compared with the poll tax, the council tax is widely accepted and understood. There are relatively few complaints from taxpayers about the structure of the tax; it is the 'experts' who mostly make the criticisms above.

6.25   The Government is very aware, however, of concerns about the perceived fairness of the tax. In looking at options for improvement, we note that changing its structure to remedy some of the concerns might result in further problems.

For example, making the tax more 'progressive' by changing the ratios could have a 'regressive' impact in some cases. For example it would raise the tax burden for pensioners in high value homes as well as key workers on modest incomes who rent their homes in property hot spots.

6.26   We will listen to the views of tax payers and local government about council tax bands and related matters. We shall introduce legislation to make it clear that additional council tax valuation bands can be created without new primary legislation.

Setting the council tax

6.27   Decisions on local taxes are a vital part of local democracy and accountability. They should be taken by the local authority, based on its assessment of the costs it faces and of local peoples' willingness to pay.

CONSULTATION

6.28   Over the last three years, the annual council tax increase for England has averaged 6.4 per cent. Over the same period, the RPI has increased by 2.1 per cent a year, earnings by 4.5 per cent, and pensions by 3.9 per cent. Local authorities face a lot of pressure from the Government and local service users to increase spend and improve services. But the

Government does not believe that council tax increases at the level seen in recent years are sustainable in the future. We think local people will refuse to accept that their authorities need to increase council tax by more than twice the rate of inflation. It is therefore in local authorities' own interests to establish their taxpayers' views on council tax increases before they take budget decisions. Evidence of how an authority has engaged local taxpayers in these difficult trade-off decisions will be an important part of the authority's performance assessment.

6.29   The evidence suggests that local people value the chance to have their say on council tax increases. This is the message from attitude surveys and from the turnout in the three referenda on council tax increases held in recent years (see below).

6.30   However, attitudes to consultation on taxation and expenditure are not straightforward. Government research showed that:

- There are concerns that, under some methods of consultation such as public meetings, voter involvement is open to excessive influence from an unrepresentative minority with an axe to grind.

- People find the present communication of financial information to be over-complex and meaningless, and that it does not answer their questions.

What the public thinks

In the British Attitudes Survey, 64% of respondents said that the council tax should be set locally, but 69% said that local authorities should hold referenda if they wish to raise council tax by more than inflation.

Year	Council	Turnout in council tax referendum	Turnout in last local election	Council tax increase supported
1999	Milton Keynes	45%	25%	10%
2001	Bristol	40%	33%	No change
2001	Croydon	35%	38%	2%

- Local authorities and residents often have different views about the strengths and weaknesses of different methods of consultation, and these should be taken into account when deciding on a package of consultation techniques.

6.31   The Government has established a consultation forum of local authority advisers, and has recently commissioned research to produce guidance on best practice in consulting local people about tax and spend decisions.

RESERVE POWERS

6.32   Local authorities are accountable to their taxpayers and voters for the council tax increases that they set, and Government is reluctant to intervene in these local decisions by placing a 'cap' on local authority budgets. This can create ambiguity about who is responsible for local tax decisions.

6.33   Ideally, our long-term goal is to dispense with the power to cap local authority budgets altogether. But, as it is local taxpayers who bear the risks, we need to proceed towards this goal cautiously. Protecting the interests of those who use and pay for local services has always been an essential plank in our reform agenda. We also note that capping may be needed to provide safeguards to ensure that the council tax revaluation does not lead to an increase in overall yield at the time of revaluation.

6.34   The first step towards our long-term goal was taken in the Local Government Act 1999, following the Government's firm manifesto commitment to abolish 'crude and universal' capping. The 1999 Act created more selective reserve powers to protect council taxpayers from excessive increases. These reserve powers can be used to cap a budget increase 'in year', to pre-specify the maximum amount which an authority can set in subsequent years, or to set a notional budget requirement for the current year against which future years' capping decisions will be taken.

6.35   Since we introduced the reserve capping powers we have been clear that they should only be used in exceptional circumstances. They have not been used against any authority in England in relation to their council tax increases in the last three years. In making decisions about the use of the reserve powers, a major consideration has been evidence of how local taxpayers have been engaged in decisions about council tax increases.

6.36   As the measures proposed elsewhere in the white paper strengthen local democracy and public engagement, the need for the reserve powers is now less pressing. We therefore propose to take a second step towards our longer term goal by not using the reserve powers against high-performing authorities. We would expect such authorities to set their tax increases responsibly and any additional expenditure by them to represent good value for money.

6.37   Over the next few years we will consider the impact of this policy on those who use and those who pay for local services. In this light, we will then consider making further progress towards our ideal goal of ending capping entirely, whilst bearing in mind the need for safeguards at the time of revaluation.

COUNCIL TAX BENEFIT SUBSIDY LIMITATION

6.38   The national taxpayer bears part of the cost of council tax increases in the form of higher council tax benefit payments. Council tax benefit subsidy limitation (CTBSL) was introduced in 1998, so that local authorities making steep council tax increases should contribute to the cost they impose on national taxpayers.

6.39 The box explains (in simplified form) how CTBSL works. The step-by-step calculations of a CTBSL liability run to 7 pages. As the green paper noted, the CTBSL scheme is complex, and widely misunderstood, often being seen by local authorities as 'capping by the back door'. It is also incompatible with the overall framework of giving local government more devolution and more local discretion.

How CTBSL works

The Government sets a guideline increase in council tax. For the last 3 years, this has been 4½% or such higher increase as permits the authority to raise its budget in line with the cash increase in its SSA.

CTBSL operates cumulatively, using the actual level of council tax in 1998-99 as the starting point. This means that, in order to calculate the guideline increase for 2001-02, an authority must work out what increase was permitted in 1999-2000 and 2000-01.

A council, where the proportion of council tax income met by benefit is at or below the national average, must contribute ⅛ of the cost of the consequential increase in the council tax benefit bill, for each ½% by which its council tax exceeds the guideline figure. This continues up to 3½% above the guideline figure, at which point the council bears the full cost of the additional council tax benefit bill. Central government continues to make a contribution to ensure that authorities where the proportion of income met by benefit is above the national average, only contribute to benefit costs as if they had the national average council tax income from benefit

6.40 There are other problems with the scheme. The impact of CTBSL on council tax is 'lumpy' and appears to vary at random. In particular, relatively small variations in spending can give rise to unpredictable financial consequences. The 4½ per cent council tax increase, above which the budget requirement has been judged to be excessive for the purposes of CTBSL, no longer has a clear rationale, and the linkage of the CTBSL guideline figure to the SSA is a misuse of SSA (see para 3.16). The cumulative approach to council tax increases since 1998-99 makes it difficult for an authority

to escape from its council tax level for that year. The inclusion in the CTBSL calculation of parish precepts – over which billing authorities have no direct control – is difficult to defend.

6.41 Although it would be possible to deal with some of the deficiencies of CTBSL by reforming it, it would still be a very complex scheme, sitting uncomfortably with the simpler system we are working towards. Changes to the scheme to address some of the criticisms might make it even more complex, and could lead to some making a contribution to benefit costs for the first time, and others paying more than previously.

6.42 The Government has concluded that it should abolish CTBSL for all authorities. This is an important step in reducing bureaucracy and the excessive regulation of council finances by central government. Abolition will lead to simplification of both the local government finance and benefits systems, and will remove a major source of instability and unpredictability from councils' budgeting processes.

Discounts and exemptions

6.43 The Government is looking to devolve more decisions on council tax discounts and exemptions. Allowing more decisions to be made locally will give local government greater flexibility to design policies appropriate to their areas and give them an ability to respond to difficult cases which are not covered by the present nationally set discounts and exemptions.

6.44 In the rural white paper, we said that we would consult on giving local authorities discretion to end the 50 per cent discount for second homes. The impact of holiday homes in some areas is a good example of how the housing market varies from place to place, and is also an example of how local authorities could potentially use the council tax to respond to local factors. Two other examples are:

- Many properties across the country are left empty for long periods of time. This has a detrimental effect on the immediate neighbourhood and often flies in the face of high local demand for housing. The reasons for properties being left empty vary – they may be due to a depressed property market or for personal reasons.

- Where flood damaged homes are left unoccupied but still furnished, their owners may still have to pay council tax for the unoccupied home as well as for any temporary accommodation.

6.45   In *Council Tax: A consultation paper on proposed changes for second homes and long term empty homes*, the Government is presently inviting views on proposals to give billing authorities discretion to remove or reduce the 50 per cent discount for second homes and long-term empty homes. It is also proposing to give billing authorities discretion to grant council tax discounts and exemptions beyond the existing national framework. This will allow them to respond to local factors such as flooding and to consider the case for tax liability in individual circumstances that are not covered by existing benefits, discounts and exemptions. This discretion to deal with individual cases is particularly important for second homes and long-term empty homes, as council tax benefit cannot be claimed for these properties.

6.46   The consultation paper proposes a range of options for using the proceeds from removing or reducing discounts for unoccupied housing. It also proposes that billing authorities should bear the full cost of any discretionary exemptions or discounts that they choose to apply in their areas.

Billing arrangements

6.47   The green paper noted that council tax bills in counties are issued by shire districts, even though county councils typically account for 80 per cent of the bill. This is potentially highly misleading. Local democratic accountability depends on voters being clear which tier of local government is responsible for the increase in their council tax bills.

6.48   However, the transfer of billing responsibilities would be disruptive. It would also only be a partial solution to the problem. It is *less* misleading if council taxpayers think the county accounts for the whole of their council tax bill, but it is still wrong. And it is just as important that council tax bills in London distinguish between the borough's charge and the GLA's charge.

6.49   We have therefore focused on reforming the presentation of council tax bills. The Government has amended the council tax billing regulations to make council tax bills more transparent. The front of the bill will show clearly how much council tax each tier of authority is charging. It will also show up-front the annual per cent increase or decrease in each authority's charge.

6.50   In *Improving Communications with Council Taxpayers: A Consultation Paper*, we invited views on a range of measures for improving the information sent out about council tax, including the information sent on and with council tax bills. It also invited views on the potential benefits of electronic billing and the practical issues raised. Electronic billing should enable taxpayers to dig beneath the surface of their bill in as much or as little detail as they want. It can also signpost them easily towards further information, such as on payment options or discounts and exemptions. The box overleaf shows how a new-style council tax bill might look.

6.51 We conclude that, for the time being, council tax and business rate bills in two tier areas in should continue to be issued by district councils, which will also remain responsible for housing and council tax benefits. However, the Government will keep this issue under review. We shall also want to see how well district councils manage the responsibilities they will acquire as billing authorities for operating council tax discounts and exemptions and promoting BIDs.

Combined fire authorities

6.52 Combined fire authorities (CFAs) operate in county areas that were affected by local government reorganisation. They draw their revenue funding as a levy from their constituent local authorities. A number of respondents to last year's local government finance green paper suggested that the financial arrangements for CFAs undermined financial accountability, and that they should be made precepting bodies. In particular, unitary authorities were concerned about their limited influence on financial decisions affecting them, as they were 'minority shareholders'.

6.53 The Government agrees that the present arrangements are haphazard and the council tax contribution to CFAs will be more transparent to taxpayers if they become major precepting authorities. The fire service is a local government function and should have accountability arrangements appropriate to that function. We will therefore take the legislative steps necessary to make CFAs major precepting authorities. In advance of this, our consultation paper *Improving Communication with Council Taxpayers* is seeking views on ways to better present taxpayers' contributions to CFAs under the current financing arrangements.

Example: Electronic council tax bill

Issued by Westfold District Council on behalf of the County Council, District Council, Police Authority and Parish Council

This is the council tax bill for 18 Marlborough Street, South Hillingham, Blankshire. Your council tax records show that the property is in **Band C** and is occupied by 2 or more adults. Your bill has been calculated on this basis and no discounts or exemptions apply. If you think this information is wrong, or wish to find out more about discounts, exemptions and council tax benefit, <u>click here</u>.

The council tax bill for your property is **£738.70**, made up as follows:

Blankshire Council Tax (Westfold Accounts)	Bill for 2003-04	Increase from 2002-03
Blankshire County Council	573.28	4.2%
Westfold District Council	112.40	8.0%
Blankshire Police Authority	26.14	8.9%
Hillingham Parish Council	26.88	22.2%
Total	738.70	5.4%

You are currently paying your council tax bill by direct debit in the form of 10 equal monthly instalments. If you wish to continue paying by this means, you need take no further action. **£73.87** will be deducted automatically in each month from April 2003 to January 2004.

For further information about the council tax, <u>click here</u>. To find out more about what your council tax pays for and what services are available, <u>click here</u>.

CHAPTER 7
The way forward on business rates

The starting point

7.1   In the past, local authorities levied a non-domestic rate on commercial properties, alongside the domestic rate on residential properties (see paragraph 6.1). They set the level of both taxes. However, in 1990, the non-domestic rate was 'nationalised'. The tax is still collected by local authorities, but the level of the tax is set nationally and the proceeds are pooled centrally and redistributed to councils on the basis of their resident population.

7.2   Each property has a rateable value, which represents its assumed annual rental value. The rateable value is assessed by the Government's Valuation Office Agency, and appeals are handled by the local valuation tribunals. The amount of business rate paid is based on a national rate per £ of rateable value, also known as the multiplier, which currently stands at 43.0 pence in England. Legislation says that this cannot rise by more than the Retail Price Index (RPI). The rate is adjusted at each revaluation so that the tax yield remains the same after revaluation as before.

7.3   Unlike council tax, the business rate is already subject to a statutory requirement that all properties be revalued once every five years. Revaluations took place in 1990, 1995 and 2000. At each of these revaluations, the Government operated a transitional relief scheme.

What the green paper said

7.4   The green paper proposed a number of reforms on the valuation side. It canvassed the idea of increasing the revaluation cycle from 5 years to 6, 8 or 10 years. It proposed that transitional relief schemes should unwind more quickly and should operate without subsidy from other taxpayers. It suggested improvements to the revaluation process to provide a better service to ratepayers. It proposed some freedom to vary the level of the business rate to take account of yield lost as a result of appeals. It proposed that the administrative support for the valuation tribunals should be established as a non-departmental public body.

7.5   The green paper also dealt with various proposals for business rate reliefs. The proposals for business rate reliefs covered small businesses, non-profit making sports clubs and rural businesses in villages, such as food stores, pubs and petrol stations.

7.6   The green paper set out in more detail the Government's proposals for a supplementary rate, which would permit authorities to levy a supplementary rate of up to 1 per cent per annum over five years. To do this, they would need to have a partnership arrangement with local business. The green paper spelled out the procedures for securing business agreement to the establishment of a partnership arrangement, for levying the supplementary rate and for sharing the proceeds between authorities.

What you said

7.7   Responses to the green paper revealed a strong consensus on the valuation issues. There was a clear preference for sticking with a five-yearly revaluation cycle with a significant minority favouring three years. With this exception, people backed the Government's proposed reforms.

7.8   There was also general support for the rate relief proposals. However, valuation experts raised legitimate questions about the likely impact of the reliefs.

7.9   The one issue on which there was a strong divergence of views was the supplementary rate. Virtually all local authority respondents supported the reform, though many felt that it did not go far enough, and would have preferred the Government to give councils full control over the business rate. Virtually all business respondents opposed the reform. Both local authority and business respondents felt that the decision-making process was too complex, but they had differing views on how it should be simplified. Local authorities favoured solutions which made the supplement easier to raise, whilst business favoured solutions which made it easier to block.

Revaluation and transitional relief

7.10   The next revaluation will go ahead as planned in 2005 and revaluations will continue to take place at five-yearly intervals. The green paper responses sent the clear message that businesses were happy with this cycle and did not want to lengthen it, e.g. by moving to an eight- or ten-year cycle. Since a five- or six-yearly cycle of council tax revaluations would be too frequent (see para 6.18), the best way of integrating the two cycles is for business rate revaluations to take place every five years and council tax revaluations every ten years. We will conduct the 2005 revaluation according to the advanced timetable proposed in the green paper. In preparation for this, the first meetings of the National Ratepayer Valuation Forum have already taken place. We will implement our proposal to decriminalise the penalty for non-return of statutory information forms, extending the completion period to 56 days. There will be a right of appeal against the new civil penalty to the valuation tribunals.

7.11   The green paper responses confirmed that transitional relief is important to many businesses. It assists them in planning ahead to know that they will not face dramatic changes in their rates bills. The Government will therefore make transitional relief a permanent feature of the business rate revaluation, in the same way that floors and ceilings will be a permanent feature of the revenue grant distribution system. However, the Government can see no reason why a transitional relief scheme for business should be subsidised by the generality of taxpayers. Accordingly, as proposed in the green paper, the transitional relief scheme needs to be self-financing. The legislation we propose to introduce will make that requirement clear. We shall also require transitional relief schemes to 'unwind' by the time of the next revaluation – i.e. each transitional relief scheme will run for no more than five years and all properties will have reached their correct rate liability by the end of the transitional relief period.

7.12   The box below shows how this could be achieved by phasing of both increases and decreases in rate bills. This example uses bills based on notional rateable values as steps between the old and the new value, for both increases and decreases, to ensure that in each year all the costs of phasing increases are fully met by phasing decreases. An alternative would be to fund the phasing of increases through a supplement on the multiplier, which would allow different approaches to be taken with the phasing of increases. But we shall want to discuss the detailed operation of a scheme with business and with valuation professionals.

Transitional relief		Year 0	Year 1	Year 2	Year 3	Year 4	Year 5
Company A	Rateable Value	100	116	122	128	134	140
	Multiplier	50.0%	46.6%	47.8%	48.9%	50.2%	51.4%
	Gross Rate Bill	£50.00	£65.23	£66.86	£68.53	£70.24	£72.00
	Transitional Relief	£0.00	£11.18	£8.60	£5.87	£3.01	£0.00
	Rates Paid	£50.00	£54.05	£58.26	£62.66	£67.23	£72.00
Company B	Rateable Value	100	110	110	110	110	110
	Multiplier	50.0%	46.6%	47.8%	48.9%	50.2%	51.4%
	Gross Rate Bill	£50.00	£51.25	£52.53	£53.84	£55.19	£56.57
	Transitional Relief	£0.00	£0.00	£0.00	£0.00	£0.00	£0.00
	Rates Paid	£50.00	£51.25	£52.53	£53.84	£55.19	£56.57
Company C	Rateable Value	100	104	98	92	86	80
	Multiplier	50.0%	46.6%	47.8%	48.9%	50.2%	51.4%
	Gross Rate Bill	£50.00	£37.27	£38.20	£39.16	£40.14	£41.14
	Transitional Relief	£0.00	−£11.18	−£8.60	−£5.87	−£3.01	£0.00
	Rates Paid	£50.00	£48.45	£46.80	£45.03	£43.15	£41.14
Total	Net Yield	£150.00	£153.75	£157.59	£161.53	£165.57	£169.71
	Growth		2.5%	2.5%	2.5%	2.5%	2.5%
	Cost of TR	£0.00	£0.00	£0.00	£0.00	£0.00	£0.00

A business rate revaluation comes into effect from 1 April of Year 1. Across England as a whole, property values increase by 10 per cent. But there is a spread of outcomes for individual properties. Company A's rateable value increases by 40 per cent, Company B's increases by 10 per cent and Company C's decreases by 20 per cent. The multiplier is reduced in year 1 to offset the increase in total rateable value and maintain total yield, and is also increased by inflation assumed to be 2½ per cent. The net effect is to reduce the multiplier from 50.0p to 46.6p. In each of the subsequent years, the multiplier increases in line with RPI, assumed to be 2½ per cent.

Under this transitional relief scheme, all properties move to a rates bill based on the new rateable value by equal increments or decrements. A notional rateable value is calculated for each year. In the first year there are two steps. The pre-revaluation year 0, RV is first increased for all properties by the average percentage increase in rateable value. The difference between this notional figure and the actual new rateable value is phased in equal steps over the 5 years of the rating lists. So in year 1, the notional RV used to calculate the bill is the year 0 RV plus the national average percentage increase plus one fifth of the difference between the notional RV and the actual new RV, which may be upwards or downwards. In each subsequent year a further fifth of that difference is added to or subtracted from the notional RV. So by year 5, immediately before the next revaluation, the scheme has fully 'unwound' and the actual RV is used to calculate the bill, so all three companies are paying an amount based on their actual rateable value with no relief. In the intervening period, Company B is unaffected by transitional relief, and its rates bill rises in line with RPI (assumed to be 2½ per cent), whilst the rates bill for Company A (a loser from the revaluation) is, in effect, subsidised by Company C (a gainer from the revaluation).

7.13 The other main change we want to make in this area is to legislate to give more flexibility in setting the multiplier to account for losses on appeal. This will protect the rate yield from unexpected losses. As now, we will estimate at the time of each revaluation the likely losses from appeal during the valuation period and build this into the multiplier at the start of the period. However, if this turns out to have been an under or over-estimate, we will be able to make subsequent adjustments to the multiplier to take account of this. Making an estimate in advance and adjusting subsequently only to the extent that the estimate was incorrect will provide businesses with greater certainty than if we simply changed the multiplier once losses became known.

7.14 As we said in *Modernising Local Government Finance: A Green Paper*, we will end prescribed assessment at the time of the next revaluation. This means that those industries that currently have their rateable values prescribed by the Secretary of State will have them assessed by the VOA like other ratepayers. They will also acquire the same right as other ratepayers to challenge their valuation.

Business Improvement Districts (BIDs)

7.15 The Government wishes to promote partnership working between authorities and local businesses. This will strengthen councils' role as community leaders, encouraging them to improve links with their business communities, while businesses will be more involved in decisions affecting their local area. There are many good examples of councils and businesses in England working closely together to tackle issues of shared concern.

7.16 The supplementary rate was intended to provide an incentive to partnership working. It did this by making the authority's power to levy the rate dependent on having in place a partnership arrangement. However, it is clear from many of the local authority responses to the green paper that the supplementary rate was seen primarily as a means of raising revenue, and that the requirement to have a partnership arrangement with local business was seen as a burden on local authorities. Many responses commented that the 'cost' of working in partnership seemed excessive in relation to the additional revenue that the supplementary rate would generate. For their part, business organisations pointed out that the only way in which local businesses could be sure that a supplementary rate would not be imposed on

them was to vote against the establishment of the partnership arrangement. There was therefore a real risk that a supplementary rate could become an obstacle to partnership working, rather than facilitating it. There was also a real risk that the supplementary rate powers would not have been used in most areas of the country.

7.17 The Government has therefore decided instead to take forward a scheme of business improvement districts (BIDs), funded through an agreed additional levy on the rates, to reflect more closely the business improvement districts which have worked well in the United States. BIDs will enable all district, borough and unitary councils to fund and take forward schemes that will benefit the local community, subject to the agreement of local ratepayers. This will also give ratepayers more say in how their rates are used. There will be considerable scope for local flexibility in how and where BIDs should be introduced. BIDs will require co-operation on specific projects, which will develop closer relations between councils and businesses, while local strategic partnerships provide a forum for broader partnership working between councils and businesses. The table below summarises the main differences between the supplementary rate and the new BID approaches.

7.18 The most significant change is that all the businesses that would be covered by a BID will have a vote on whether or not it is introduced. If they want it, the BID will happen. If they don't want it, it won't. It will be necessary for the Government to lay down the basic rules that govern the vote. But almost every other aspect of a BID proposal should be settled between authorities and local businesses.

7.19 The starting point in establishing a BID will be the identification of a gap or weakness in the services provided by local authorities, which is a source of concern to local businesses. In America, BIDs often focus on the problems of a run-down or unsafe town centre, where businesses are prepared to pay increased taxes to secure preventative measures (more frequent policing, installation of CCTV cameras and litter bins), remedial measures (a rapid response to graffiti and litter, replacing street lamps, mending pavements) and investment in the visual appearance of the area (new street furniture, tree-planting, etc). But the same approach can be applied to other types of problem – by providing local training and employment schemes or funding a more frequent rural bus service. The important point is that both parties – the authority and business community – are clear what problem they want tackled and what specific measures they want taken to deal with it.

7.20 In these circumstances, it is clearly inappropriate to legislate on the scope or cost of a BID. It can be as modest or ambitious as local businesses want. The geographical boundaries of a BID area will be decided locally, as part of the BID proposal. It could be focussed on a very small area such as a high street, or a slightly wider area, or it could cover the whole of a local authority. Whatever the area proposed, all ratepayers in that area will have a vote on the proposed BID.

7.21 BIDs could also cross local authority boundaries, for example in urban areas where borough boundaries do not exactly match local communities. In such cases, one authority would

	Supplementary rate	BID
Duration	The supplement would be reviewed after 5 years.	There is no time limit to the BID arrangement, but business endorsement will need to be renewed after no more than 5 years, or sooner if agreed locally.
Level	The supplement could not increase by more than 1 per cent a year up to a maximum of 5 per cent.	There is no limit. The council and local business will decide for themselves the amount and form of the BID levy.
Responsible Authority	Any local authority could levy the supplementary rate. There would be arrangements for sharing the supplement between district and county councils, and between London boroughs and the GLA.	The BID levy can only be raised by the billing authority. Other public, private or voluntary sector bodies are brought in on the basis of what they contribute to the BID.
Decision Making	In order to levy a supplementary rate, the authority must establish a partnership arrangement (PA) with local business. Businesses vote on whether to have a PA. The authority could ask the Secretary of State to overturn the vote outcome, eg if a supplementary rate proposal was rejected on the basis of a very low turnout. The authority could levy the supplementary rate without the agreement of its PA, but would have to surrender the proceeds into the national pot. The authority would need the PA's agreement in order to retain the proceeds.	All ratepayers covered by the BID vote on whether to have a levy. The vote would be on a full BID proposal, including the amount to be raised, what it was to be used for and how the project would be managed, and the role of and contributions from other bodies such as property owners, county and parish councils, and any RDA or European funding. The outcome of the vote is binding on all parties. The council can veto the vote if it can demonstrate the BID conflicts with local interests set out in statutory plans. Ratepayers could appeal to the Secretary of State against a council veto.
Initiation	The local authority would initiate the supplementary rate proposal.	A referendum can be called by the authority or by local businesses.

be designated to lead the council side of the BID partnership. This could be the one containing the greatest part of the BID area by rateable value, but a different authority could lead if agreed locally. A majority vote would be needed in each local authority part of the BID area. If a majority were not secured in all authorities within the BID area, the BID could proceed in those authority parts where there was a majority.

7.22   It is important that businesses are confident that a BID scheme can be terminated if it is not delivering. Against that, they have to weigh the fact that authorities will be reluctant to make a capital investment unless they are confident of ongoing revenue support. It will generally be appropriate for the BID mandate to be reviewed after five years, but that may not fit all cases. For example, the authority and local businesses may feel that it makes sense to start with a modest BID with a business rate mandate renewed annually, and then move on – if the initial scheme works well – to a more ambitious and longer-term scheme, once trust has been built up on both sides.

7.23   Local businesses will want to ensure that the BID levy secures a genuine addition to the services they get from their local authority, rather than subsidising existing services. But there is no need to legislate on this. It will be up to the authority to satisfy businesses on this score. If they fail to do so, businesses will not support the BID.

7.24   Businesses may want to participate in or lead the running of the BID, as often happens in America and with existing voluntary schemes in England. The Government would warmly welcome this. Authorities could gain a lot from harnessing private sector project management skills, and participating businesses could gain a better understanding of the complex issues with which their authorities are wrestling. If participating or leading in the running of a BID

is important to businesses, they will insist on it. If it is unimportant, they will not.

7.25   The legislation will make the billing authority responsible for promoting the BID on the local government side, since it is responsible for collecting the BID levy through the business rate. The participation of other bodies will depend on the contribution they can make to the BID. Because the BID levy exists purely to support the BID, no other tier of local government will have access to revenue from the levy unless it contributes to delivery of the BID.

7.26   Under this approach, the key requirement of the legislation is that it specifies very clearly the rules governing the initial vote to raise a levy to support a BID. The Government proposes two such rules:

- All occupiers of rateable business premises (hereditaments) within the BID area, who will pay the BID levy, are eligible to vote. This will inevitably include a few premises that are not businesses in the conventional sense of the word – e.g. offices occupied by Government departments, non-profit making organisations or poster sites. But we are concerned not to become embroiled in excluding premises from the list, because there are numerous marginal hard cases, because exclusions undermine the simplicity of the scheme, and because they also erode the principle that all those who pay the tax should have a say on whether it is levied.

- The introduction of the BID levy requires a simple majority of those voting **plus** a majority by rateable value of hereditament of those voting. This means that a scheme cannot be forced through by small firms against the wishes of large ones, or *vice versa*.

7.27   The legislation will permit the BID levy to be raised only on specified classes of businesses. This facilitates the sort of BID which might be of interest to retailers, say, but not to other businesses. In this case, only the businesses that would pay the levy would be eligible to vote on its introduction. The legislation will not determine the amount paid by each ratepayer. This will be for local agreement as part of the package voted on. It could be a simple percentage of rateable value, or of the rate bill net of reliefs, or it could be a fixed amount for all ratepayers. The levy could be at lower rates for different businesses, such as small firms, or those more remote from the core of the BID area, or by type of business.

7.28   We would expect successful proposals to emerge from partnerships of the council and businesses. But the legislation will allow either side to put a BID proposal to the vote. To prevent unnecessary votes on proposals with no prospect of majority support, ratepayer proposals would first need to be supported by a proportion of those within the BID area, perhaps in the range 5 per cent to 10 per cent of those affected, by number or by rateable value. A further safeguard would be to require the costs of arranging a lost vote to be met by those proposing it.

7.29   The vote would allow ratepayers to veto a BID proposal they did not like. Councils would also have reserve powers to veto proposals, where they could demonstrate that the proposed BID would conflict with locally adopted plans made under statute, or otherwise formally adopted by the council, such as the community strategy. The veto could be used where a BID proposal would cause problems elsewhere, perhaps by encouraging unsustainable traffic generation. The council veto should not normally be needed, but it provides a safeguard to prevent BIDs from harming the interests of the wider community.

7.30   Where the council veto was used, ratepayers could appeal to the Secretary of State, who could overrule the veto. This will ensure the veto is not used simply because the council does not want to support a viable BID proposal. The Secretary of State would consider the views of both the council and the ratepayers who supported the BID. The council would have to demonstrate that in exercising the veto it was acting reasonably and in the interests of the wider local community.

7.31   Discussions with local government and national bodies representing businesses have welcomed the BID concept and the Government's intention to adopt a 'light touch' approach to legislation. All parties see a clear need for guidance on BIDs, so that local authorities and their business communities do not have to resolve every issue from scratch. But they agreed that there is no reason why this guidance should not be drawn up by local authority and business organisations, instead of by Government. In this way, the BID concept is 'owned' by business and local government at the national level, as well as at the local level. The guidance can draw on the best practice already developed in existing voluntary BID schemes.

7.32   Those discussions have raised the issue of the role of property owners in BIDs. Property owners take a leading role in many of the voluntary BID schemes in England. In America, the BID levy is paid by the owners, rather than by the occupiers. However, American property taxes are generally levied on ownership, while the English rating system is a tax on property occupation. Some businesses have expressed concern that limiting the BID levy to occupiers, through the rating system, would be unfair, as much of the benefit would in fact fall to property owners, as the improvements to the area would increase property values, enabling them to increase rents to occupiers. Some fear that they would pay twice for the improvements, both through the BID levy and in the longer term through higher rents, which might force some to leave the improved area for which they had paid.

7.33   Property owners have a key role to play in BIDs. But there are significant practical difficulties in extending a BID levy to property owners, outside the rating system. This would, in effect, be a new tax on property ownership. We therefore intend to build voluntary landlord contributions, already substantial in many existing projects, into the model for BIDs in England. This would be done through the guidance rather than legislation. This will encourage BID partnerships to involve property owners from the start so that they can participate in the development and implementation of BID proposals.

7.34   The BID proposal on which ratepayers vote will show the role of property owners, including their financial and other contributions to the scheme. If occupiers are not satisfied that landlords are making a sufficient contribution, they can vote against the proposal. This will encourage the landlords to meet the concerns of occupiers if they are both to get the benefits of the scheme. This would preferably be considered as the proposal is developed and before a vote was held, but the vote will ensure that only BIDs that are acceptable to occupiers will go ahead.

7.35   The same approach can be taken with other contributors to the BID. The package voted on will include any financial and other contributions from the billing authority, other local authorities such as county or parish councils, and other sources of funding such as those provided by RDAs and European Union sources. These already play a part in some of the existing BID-type schemes. These sources of funding, together with voluntary contributions from both property owners and occupiers, will

also help to fund the BID in its preparatory stages, before the vote is held and the BID levy can be raised through the rating system.

Rate reliefs

7.36   There are several different rate reliefs currently in operation, in addition to the transitional relief scheme. Empty properties receive 50 per cent or 100 per cent mandatory relief. Charities receive 80 per cent mandatory relief, which local authorities can top up to 100 per cent. Councils can also give up to 100 per cent discretionary relief to a range of other non-profit making bodies, including sports clubs, and to any ratepayers suffering hardship. The village shop rate relief scheme provides 50 per cent mandatory relief to sole small general stores, post offices, pubs and petrol stations and all small food shops in isolated rural communities. Councils can top this relief up to 100 per cent and can provide 100 per cent discretionary relief to any small village business.

7.37   Since publishing the green paper, the village shop rate relief scheme has been extended to sole small pubs and petrol stations on 5 April 2001 and to all small food shops on 15 August 2001. Furthermore, the Rating (Former Agricultural Premises and Rural Shops) Act 2001 introduced a time-limited rate relief scheme for new, small-scale farm diversification enterprises from 15 August 2001. This also provides 50 per cent mandatory relief and a 100 per cent top up for businesses newly established in small properties that previously benefited from the agricultural exemption from rates.

7.38   It is important to set the benefits of rate reliefs in their proper perspective. Some responses to the green paper over-estimated their impact, whilst others were too dismissive.

7.39   On average, the business rate accounts for between about 10 per cent and 15 per cent of the total costs of a small firm. So, a 50 per cent reduction in the rates bill will cut the costs of the company by between 5 per cent and 7½ per cent. That is not a huge gain. It will not fundamentally transform the prospects of a small firm or a rural business that is in serious financial difficulty. However, it is big enough to make a real difference to some firms. And, of course, the rate reliefs are only one element of a broader package of measures to stimulate rural economies and foster village communities.

7.40   In their green paper responses, valuation professionals argued that the gain to the business that receives the relief will often be short-lived. Most business premises are rented. At the rent review, or on a change of occupation, the landlord will take account of the rate reduction in setting the rent. Other things being equal, landlords will seek to increase the rent on properties occupied by businesses which receive rate relief. This could leave the business no better off than it was before. In effect, the rate relief goes to landlords, not businesses. The Government believes that the property market is more complex, rational and efficient than this analysis suggests. In the rent review, landlords will take a view on the return they require on their investment, on the rent that the current tenant can afford and on the rent that possible alternative tenants might be able to afford. We have tried to focus our rate reliefs on categories of business where these factors will work to reduce the 'leakage' of benefit from the business to the landlord. A substantial minority of properties is owner-occupied, especially at the smaller end of the scale and in rural areas. Nevertheless, the Government recognises – and DTLR research confirms – that some 'leakage' is inevitable. As we said in the green paper, we shall monitor closely the effectiveness of the rate reliefs.

RATE RELIEF FOR SMALL BUSINESSES

7.41   We intend to implement the rate relief scheme for all small businesses, as proposed in the green paper. Mandatory rate relief would be available at 50 per cent for properties up to £3,000 rateable value, and would then decline on a sliding scale as rateable value increased, reaching no relief at £8,000 rateable value. Between £3,000 and £8,000, relief would decrease by 0.01 per cent for each extra £1 in rateable value – equivalent to 5 per cent per £500 or 10 per cent per £1,000. So for example at £4,500 rateable value relief would be 35 per cent, while at £6,000 rateable value, relief would be 20 per cent.

7.42   Where properties that get the new relief are also eligible for other mandatory or discretionary reliefs at a higher level they will receive the higher amount of relief. Other mandatory reliefs, including those for charities, certain village shops, new farm diversification enterprises and stud farms are all worth the same or more than relief under the small business rate relief scheme. Businesses will continue to receive these mandatory reliefs, where eligible, rather than the small business relief.

7.43   Other reliefs are available at the discretion of the local authority, including non-profit making bodies such as community sports clubs, certain village businesses that do not qualify for mandatory village shop relief, and businesses suffering hardship. These discretionary reliefs will be available in addition to the mandatory small business rate relief, acting as a top up where the council considers that discretionary relief is needed.

7.44   We have discussed with business and local authority representatives how best to implement the scheme, including how to target it on small businesses rather than small properties. Both businesses and councils saw the need for such targeting, provided it was relatively simple to apply, both for ratepayers and for billing authorities. The green paper suggested various ways to target the relief, including taking account of turnover, employers' National Insurance Contributions, or excluding certain types of property clearly not occupied by small firms, such as telecommunications masts. We have considered these, but all would involve considerable effort by both ratepayers and billing authorities to show that any criteria had been met. And neither turnover nor National Insurance Contributions guarantee an accurate measure of the smallness of a business.

7.45 We have therefore decided that the relief will be available to any business that declares to the local authority that it occupies only the one property for which it is claiming relief. This will be simple to administer for both sides, and will be similar to council tax discounts and exemptions for single persons and students. There will be no need to exclude specified types of property. This approach will clearly exclude national, regional or even local chains that occupy several small properties, ensuring that only genuine small businesses get the relief.

7.46 As we said in the green paper, this relief will be funded by a small supplement paid by all ratepayers not receiving the relief. If the relief applied to all properties below the rateable value threshold (excluding telecommunications equipment, advertising rights and car parking spaces), the supplement would add 1.1p to the 2000-01 multiplier of 43.0p, increasing rate bills by 2½ per cent for the 650,000 properties not getting relief, around 40 per cent of all non-domestic properties in England. However, targeting relief on singly occupied properties in the way proposed would significantly reduce the costs of the scheme, reducing the supplement paid by other ratepayers, although it would be paid by a larger number of ratepayers.

RATE RELIEF IN DEPRIVED URBAN AREAS

7.47 The green paper also asked whether rate relief was needed for small shops in deprived urban areas, as suggested by the Urban Task Force report in 1999. Responses to the green paper welcomed the prospect of rate relief for such businesses. They will receive such relief through the scheme that will apply to all small businesses. This will provide up to 50 per cent mandatory relief, without needing the added complexity of identifying specific types of business or urban areas.

RATE RELIEF FOR SMALL NON-PROFIT MAKING BODIES, INCLUDING SPORTS CLUBS

7.48 This new rate relief scheme will extend to small non-profit making bodies, as well as to small businesses. There is no reason why such bodies should pay higher rates than a business in a similar property. Non-profit making bodies, including voluntary sports clubs as well as philanthropic, social, fine arts and literary bodies, will for the first time be eligible for up to 50 per cent mandatory relief. As mentioned above, they will remain, as now, eligible for up to 100 per cent discretionary relief as a top up to the new mandatory relief. Where such bodies become eligible for the new relief, there is no reason to expect local authorities to withdraw or reduce discretionary relief that is currently given. The new relief will reduce local authorities' costs of funding the discretionary relief, which may allow them to increase the discretionary amount given to top up the new mandatory relief.

7.49 As promised in the green paper, we will issue revised guidance to local authorities on this discretionary relief and on the mandatory relief for charities, which was last issued in 1989. This new guidance will make clearer to local authorities the grounds on which they can exercise their discretion in granting relief to non-profit making bodies. It will also clarify the qualifying criteria for the mandatory charity relief, especially in regard to charity shops. This will help to ensure greater consistency of approach by local authorities across England. We will shortly be consulting on a draft of the new guidance.

7.50   On 30 November 2001 the Charity Commission announced that Community Amateur Sports Clubs could now apply for charitable status. They will now recognise as charitable purposes: the promotion of community participation in healthy recreation by the provision of facilities for the playing of particular sports; and the advancement of the physical education of young people not undergoing formal education. The Commission's decision does not mean that all organisations describing themselves as community sports clubs are now necessarily charitable. Along with the general requirements of charitable status, a community sports club seeking charitable status on this basis will need to make its facilities available to all members of the public who wish to use them, regardless of their levels of skill. And the sport concerned must be one that is capable of improving health or fitness.

7.51   Community sports clubs which meet the new criteria for charitable status can benefit from the mandatory 80 per cent rate relief which is already available for all premises used wholly or mainly for charitable purposes. Local authorities have the discretion to top this up to 100 per cent relief. Any non-profit making sports clubs that do not meet this expanded definition of charitable purposes remain eligible for the existing 100 per cent discretionary rate relief. They could also benefit from the new mandatory relief of up to 50 per cent proposed for small businesses and non-profit making bodies, where they fall within the rateable value limits of that scheme.

AGRICULTURAL EXEMPTION FROM RATES

7.52   On 16 February 2001 we issued a consultation paper proposing that the agricultural exemption from rates should be extended so that it covers a range of flexible farming business arrangements such as share farming, contract farming and machinery rings, where these do not currently qualify for the exemption. Responses to the consultation broadly welcomed this proposal. We will implement that revision to the exemption, to facilitate modern farm business practices.

7.53   We also intend to amend the agricultural exemption to ensure it is properly targeted on agricultural activities. Current legislation allows the exemption to premises used for ancillary activities such as food processing or packaging, provided the occupier is a company that includes some occupiers of related agricultural land. The premises need not be located on or even near a farm. A number of food processing and packaging companies not themselves engaged in agricultural activities have exploited the exemption by giving farmers shares in the company, the shares in fact being of minimal value and of no benefit to the farmers. We intend to amend the legislation so that the exemption of such ancillary premises is allowed only where the occupying company is controlled by occupiers of related agricultural premises. We will consult further on this proposal.

FUNDING OF HARDSHIP RELIEF

7.54   Local authorities have discretionary powers to grant up to 100 per cent rate relief to any business that is suffering hardship. During 2001, this power has been widely used to help businesses badly affected by the outbreak of foot and mouth disease. Local authorities meet part of the costs of hardship rate relief, to reflect the benefit it brings to the wider community. This is set at 25 per cent, in the regulations governing local authorities' contributions to the national rate pool. The legislation requires that amendments to these regulations to be made by 31 December before the start of the financial year concerned, so councils know their financial position for the forthcoming year.

7.55 Because foot and mouth disease had a significant impact in certain rural areas, the costs of hardship rate relief were much higher than expected, putting a strain on the resources of the mainly small rural districts concerned. The Government therefore provided extra funds, reducing rural local authorities' contribution to the costs of hardship relief to 5 per cent and in some cases 2 per cent of the relief given to smaller businesses. Because the pool regulations for the year had to be made the previous December, the only way we could provide this extra funding was through a separate special grant.

7.56 We intend to amend the legislation so that if in future other emergencies occur which place a burden on certain local authorities, we can increase the Government's contribution to rate relief costs during the year concerned, by amending the pool regulations. This will avoid having to set up a separate procedure to administer a special grant, which places a burden on both local and central government. The requirement to make pool regulations by the preceding December will remain, to maintain certainty for councils. Any subsequent changes can only be to increase the Government's contribution to relief, not to decrease it. This will ensure that the amended provision cannot be used to place extra costs on councils during the financial year concerned.

Valuation Tribunals

7.57 The green paper responses to the proposal for a national non-departmental public body (NDPB) to provide administrative support for the valuation tribunals (VTs) in England received general support and the Government proposes to introduce legislation at the earliest opportunity to establish the NDPB, to be known as the Valuation Tribunal Administrative Support Service.

7.58 Some respondents expressed concern about the role and composition of the NDPB's Board. The Board's role will be to provide the VTs with the necessary support and facilities to carry out their primary function of hearing and determining appeals with independence and efficiency, and to improve effectiveness by ensuring that all tribunals operate to best practice principles. It is our intention that the Board will comprise between 6 and 10 members appointed by the Secretary of State, including the Chairman and Deputy Chairman. The majority of the Board will be drawn from presidents and chairmen of VTs. The Chief Executive will be appointed by the Board, but with the approval of the Secretary of State.

7.59 In July 2001, the Lord Chancellor's Department issued a consultation paper, *Tribunals for Users*, following the review of tribunals by Sir Andrew Leggatt. This sought views on, among other things, the establishment of a unified tribunal service to include the valuation tribunals. The consultation closed on 30 November 2001. Our proposals for the VTs would be a step towards the creation of a new unified tribunal service, should that be the Government's preferred way forward.

CHAPTER 8
The way forward on other taxes and charges

The starting point

8.1   Local authorities secure most of their funding from Government grant, supplemented by council tax. However, they also raise over £6 billion through fees and charges, equivalent to 11 per cent of income from all sources. For some authorities, the proportion is much higher. But authorities are subject to arbitrary restrictions on what they can and cannot charge for.

What the green paper said

8.2   We said that charging was an important option which authorities should explore when reviewing discretionary services under best value. They should develop corporate charging policies, consult on them locally and keep them under review. We also said that we intended to make regulations under existing legislation to enable local authorities to charge for discretionary services (i.e. services that they are under no obligation to provide), but that we would consider in the light of consultation whether additional powers were needed to issue statutory guidance on charging, and that in the longer term the Government would review its policy on charges for mandatory services.

What you said

8.3   There was significant support from local authorities for the proposal that they should be given the power to charge for discretionary services. There were also calls from authorities for a wide-ranging review of charges where the level of the charge was currently fixed by legislation. Some of those who would have to pay the new charges expressed concern at the proposal: they did not want authorities to charge for general services that businesses perceive as being paid for from business rates. Charges would be acceptable only where there was a good level of service.

The Government's approach

8.4   Local authorities are responsible for only one local tax, the council tax, which currently funds 22 per cent of their expenditure. In addition, they have limited discretion over fees and charges and trading activities. It is often argued that this balance between national and local taxes has an adverse impact on local authorities' autonomy, but (as we say in chapter 2) there is little hard evidence for or against this view, and there is no consensus on how the balance might be shifted. Once we have done some further analysis of this, we shall establish a high-level working group, involving Ministers and senior figures from local government, to look at all aspects of the question, reviewing the evidence and looking at reform options. We do not think there are any quick or easy ways of securing a major shift in the balance of funding, particularly given the need to respect the views of taxpayers and to ensure that financial reform does not become a distraction from the delivery agenda. However, we need to be clear what the longer-term reform options are. We also need to consider whether there are more modest reform options that could precede these. In the meantime, we believe there is scope for embarking on a programme of reforms which are not aimed at shifting the balance of funding, but at broadening the sources of revenue available to authorities from fees and charges and from penalties, and giving them greater freedom to decide how these revenues are spent. As we say earlier in the white paper, our aim is to give councils more space to innovate, to respond in ways that are appropriate to local circumstances and to provide more effective leadership.

8.5   We shall use section 16 of the Local Government Act, to allow best value authorities to supply goods and services under contract to others in the public, private and voluntary sectors and to charge for these. There will be statutory guidance on the use of these powers. Councils should be able to trade in any service in which they have a strong performance on delivery. High performers should be able to trade across the full range of their services.

8.6   We shall use the same powers to permit authorities to charge for services they have discretion to provide. We shall allow local authorities to use the proceeds from fines on littering and dog fouling for additional spending to enhance the local environment. Subject to the necessary legislative changes and associated consultation, we also intend to allow authorities to apply the revenue from parking fines for environmental as well as transport purposes. We propose that high-performing authorities should have complete freedom to choose how littering, dog fouling and parking fines are spent. We shall review other new and existing powers to levy civil penalties with a presumption that further freedoms can be offered to high-performing authorities. An exception to these proposals will be congestion charging, which has been ring-fenced for local transport for at least ten years.

8.7   We would expect authorities to consult residents and local partners about the use of these new powers. We shall not legislate to require this, but consultation is one of the key features of good local authority financial performance, as set out in Chapter 10. The revenue from fees and charges and from penalties should not be subject to any form of resource equalisation.

Trading powers

8.8   In March, we published a consultation paper with proposals for using powers under section 16 of the Local Government Act 1999 to allow best value authorities to supply goods and services under contract to others in the public, private and voluntary sectors and to charge for these. The proposals were intended largely to replace the Local Authorities (Goods and Services) Act 1970, which allows local authorities to trade with other local authorities and designated 'public bodies'. We will build on proposals in the consultation paper and provide wider powers to trade for all authorities, when this helps achieve best value. Trading will not be subject to any centrally imposed financial limit or limited to the exploitation of existing assets, as had been proposed in the consultation paper. Councils should be able to trade in any service in which they have a strong performance on delivery. High-performers should be able to trade across the full range of their services. We will provide incentives to good service providers to take on new work and thus build their capacity to provide services to others. We will publish statutory guidance on the use of these powers, which will provide the necessary safeguards for taxpayers, local service users and businesses. This guidance will be tailored to the effectiveness of each council, giving the best performers the widest freedom and flexibility to use the powers.

Fees and charges

8.9   As well as trading under contract with others, local authorities also have limited powers to charge for some of the services they provide. It is important to distinguish between two very different types of local authority service: those which local authorities are required to provide (statutory services); and those which they have discretion to provide (discretionary services). They raise different issues.

8.10   Charges for some statutory services are set by Government. Charges for others are set by authorities. For some of the charges set by

Government, local authorities are concerned that they are set at too low a level to cover costs. For some of the charges set by local authorities, users of the services are concerned about the inexplicably wide variations in the charges which different authorities make. For instance, the Royal Commission on Long Term Care and the Audit Commission both identified problems with the variations in home care charging policies between local councils. As a result, the Department of Health has recently issued statutory guidance to local authorities on fairer charging policies for home care and other non-residential social services.

8.11   The general power in the Local Government Act 2000 to promote the economic, social and environmental well-being of local communities gives authorities very broad discretion to provide services, but does not provide a power to charge. In addition, there are numerous statutory restrictions on their existing ability to charge. Public health legislation prohibits authorities from charging for men's urinals. There is no such restriction on charging for women's toilets. But most authorities have concluded that it is indefensible to discriminate between the genders, and probably inconsistent with equal rights and human rights legislation. This has led at least one authority to abandon its plans to pay for service improvements to public lavatories by charging for entry to a small number of them in areas frequented by tourists. If the authority cannot justify or afford the cost of providing a free service, it will not provide it at all. The Audit Commission drew attention to this example in their 1999 report *The Price is Right?* It illustrates a more general problem. There are a variety of services which cannot be operated on a commercial basis, but which an authority could provide if it were allowed to recover some of the cost via a fee or charge. A number of authorities included their graveyards and

crematoria in the first round of best value reviews. They often found that their charges were excessive or inadequate, bearing little relation to the cost of the service, but they also found that the range of services they could provide to the bereaved was constrained by their inability to make a charge. As the best value reviews proceed, more such cases are likely to emerge.

8.12   We said in the green paper that we endorsed the Audit Commission's view that, in general, if authorities have discretion on whether or not to provide a service, they should also have discretion on whether or not to charge for it. Under section 150 of the Local Government and Housing Act 1989, the Government can make regulations allowing authorities to charge for specified matters. However, neither the 1989 Act nor the Local Government Act 2000 can be used to create a general power to charge for services. We therefore propose to use the powers under section 16 of the Local Government Act 1999 to make an order which gives all local authorities a general power to charge for discretionary services which they already have powers to provide. We will consult on a draft order, which will set conditions limiting how much can be charged and which may specify exceptions to the general power to charge. The effect is to shift the burden of proof. Instead of authorities having to make a case to be allowed to charge for a particular service, the onus will be on those who believe that authorities should not have the power to charge for it. We aim to have the order in place by July 2002.

Penalties

8.13   In the negotiations of local PSAs with Middlesbrough, Newcastle upon Tyne and Stockton-on-Tees, the Government agreed that the authorities should be able to tackle littering and dog fouling more effectively by having the income from these penalties returned to them in a grant that they can use for street cleaning and local environmental projects. With this help, the authorities are planning to achieve more demanding targets for the improvement of the local environment than they would otherwise have thought possible.

8.14   From April 2002, the fixed penalty for littering and dog fouling will be increased from £25 to £50. We shall allow local authorities to use the proceeds from fines on littering and dog fouling for additional spending to enhance the local environment.

8.15   Local authorities which have taken on decriminalised parking enforcement are already permitted to retain the proceeds from parking fines. At present, they are required to use the proceeds for transport purposes. Subject to the necessary legislative changes and associated consultation, we intend to allow them to use the proceeds from parking fines to support local environmental improvements. We propose to allow high-performing authorities complete freedom to choose how the money from littering, dog fouling and parking fines is spent. In addition, we shall review other new and existing powers to levy civil penalties, with a presumption that further freedoms can be offered to high-performing authorities.

8.16   It is important that authorities do not become dependent on income from penalties to support their mainstream services and that they do not lose sight of the primary purpose of the penalties. The main purpose of introducing penalties for littering, dog fouling, or illegal parking is to discourage these behaviours. They are not intended primarily to generate income. Indeed, if they were wholly successful in securing compliance with the law, they would generate no revenue at all.

Managing liberalisation

8.17   In general, the Government believes that local authority income sources should not be hypothecated. There are a few exceptions to this rule. For example, we have made it clear that every penny of the net proceeds from road user charges and levies on workplace parking will be retained locally and ring-fenced for improving local transport for at least 10 years. Similarly, the purpose of having a separate housing revenue account is to demonstrate that the income from rents is spent on housing. However, in the vast majority of cases, local authorities are free to spend the income raised from fees and charges as they wish.

8.18   We also see a general need to give authorities greater freedom to support worthwhile local services and initiatives, and make them slightly less reliant on council tax. Liberalisation of trading, and fees and charges for discretionary services, is the way forward in the short term.

8.19   The ability of different authorities to raise income from the new revenue sources will vary considerably. A core city or central London borough is likely to be able to raise much more income from the penalties at paragraph 8.15 than authorities in rural areas. The Government does not see a case for complicating the local government finance system by introducing new forms of resource equalisation to deal with this. Equalisation would not reward high-performing authorities.

8.20   It will be important that councils win and retain the trust of those who pay the charges and penalties. They need to consult in advance about their revenue-raising plans, and about how the additional funds will be spent. They need to demonstrate to voters and businesses that they will get value for money from the additional expenditure, and that the new powers will be exercised responsibly.

CHAPTER 9
The way forward for parishes

The starting point

9.1   There are about 8,700 parish and town councils – referred to collectively as 'parishes' from this point – in England. They vary widely in many ways. Some represent hamlets of fewer than 100 people. Others represent larger towns, with populations of up to 70,000. Their annual budgets range from under £100 to over £1 million. The role they play also varies widely. Some play a very modest and local role, but others are more active, with a role very similar to that of some of the smaller district councils.

9.2   The number of parishes has increased recently. Over eighty new ones have been created in England since 1997. Parishes have also been given some new powers recently. These include powers to provide community transport, traffic calming and crime prevention measures under the Local Government and Rating Act 1997. In addition, several measures for strengthening the role of parishes were announced in the rural white paper: *Our countryside: the future, a fair deal for rural England* in November 2000. The most prominent of

these was the introduction of the concept of 'Quality Parish and Town Councils', on which a consultation paper was issued jointly by central and local government on 7 November.

9.3   Parishes spend much less, and raise much less in tax, than principal authorities. But there are many more of them, and they have more councillors overall than principal authorities. Further comparisons between parishes and principal authorities are given in the table below.

What the green paper said

9.4   The green paper aimed to promote a debate about the funding of parishes. It suggested that the present financial arrangements for parishes work well. But it wished to establish whether there was scope to improve the system, to make it more responsive to the current needs and future aspirations of the councils – particularly the larger ones – and of the people who use and pay for the services which they provide.

Comparing parish and town councils and principal authorities in England		
	Parish and town councils	Principal authorities
Number	approx. 8,700	432
Population covered: Number	15 million	50 million
% of England total	30%	100%
Aggregate budgeted spending in 2001-02	£290 million	£60,300 million
Spending in 2001-02 funded by council tax	£193 million	£15,200 million
Spending funded by council tax as % of aggregate budgeted spending in 2001-02	67%	25%
Aggregate budgeted spending per resident in 2001-02	£20	£1,200

Notes:
1. Most of the figures for parish and town councils are estimates.
2. Some of the population and spending shown for parish and town councils is in parished areas where there is not a parish or town council. Such areas have a parish meeting instead. There are about 1,500 parish meetings in England.
3. The population in parished areas comprises about half of the population of England outside London and metropolitan areas. There are only a few parished areas in metropolitan areas, and none in London.

9.5   It highlighted some aspects of the existing financial regime for parishes which do not work well, such as the treatment of parish precepts under the council tax benefit subsidy limitation scheme and the unfairness of double taxation. It also pointed to other aspects which may need rethinking in the light of changes proposed for principal authorities, such as controls on borrowing. Finally, it posed several specific questions about the financial regime for larger parishes.

What you said

9.6   There was a high level of interest in the section of the green paper that covered parishes. We are pleased that they took the opportunity to engage closely with the debate.

9.7   Respondents could be divided broadly into two categories:

- Those who were content with the existing system and proposed only minor changes. Their biggest concerns were audit and double taxation (which is described in paragraph 9.21). They were mostly small and medium-sized parishes.

- Larger parishes, particularly those with an average annual income of over £500,000, which are subject to best value. They tended to recommend more radical measures – such as the replacement of section 137 of the Local Government Act 1972 with a general power to incur expenditure and a share of direct government grant via the business rate or revenue support grant.

The Government's approach

9.8   We believe that parishes form an important tier of local government at a 'grassroots' level, close to the people. We believe also that they should be free to play a key role in leading and empowering their local communities. It is important, therefore, that we make the financial arrangements for parishes more responsive to their current needs and aspirations – and those of the people who use and pay for the services which they provide. In identifying a way forward, we have tried to address concerns of both groups of respondents described above. Some improvements can be made that benefit all parishes. But it is also clear that a 'one size fits all' approach to the parishes' financial regime is not tenable when looking at councils which vary to the extent described at paragraph 9.1.

9.9   We want to work with parishes to help them realise their potential. Many parishes themselves want to do more, and some are already making use of the opportunities they now have. We need to ensure that the financial framework does not impede them – and frees them wherever possible. However, as with principal authorities, we must ensure that interests of people who use and pay for local services are protected. The white paper proposals do this, creating a modernised regime that helps all parishes move towards Quality Parish and Town Council status, while allowing extra flexibilities and funding for best value parishes.

The Government's proposals

9.10   Our key measures are:

- To legislate to **increase the ceiling on section 137 expenditure to £5 per elector and then raise it annually in line with inflation** (see paragraphs 9.16 to 9.18);

- **To issue good practice guidance to promote the avoidance of double taxation** (see paragraphs 9.21 to 9.22);

- **To make it possible for parish councillors to authorise payments by their parish using electronic methods** (see paragraphs 9.23 to 9.24);

- **To improve the borrowing approval system by removing the annual fixed limit, streamlining the application process, and by clarifying and advertising the criteria more widely** (see paragraphs 9.25 to 9.29);

- **To pay a grant from central government to the best value parishes** (see paragraph 9.31);

- **To give best value parishes a general power to charge for discretionary services** (see paragraph 9.32).

9.11   In addition, the treatment of parish precepts under the council tax benefit subsidy limitation scheme will no longer be a problem. This is because we have decided to abolish the scheme altogether from the next financial year, 2002-03. Further details are given in chapter 6.

9.12   Parishes will be able to participate in business improvement district (BID) partnerships in their area. Further details are given in chapter 7. BIDs will be funded through an agreed additional levy on the business rate, to reflect more closely the business improvement districts which have worked well in the United States. There will be considerable scope for local flexibility in how and where BIDs should be introduced. Whilst billing authorities and business ratepayers would be in the lead in BID partnerships, parishes are likely to be well-placed to be key partners in some areas, playing an important role in agreeing and delivering the projects that business ratepayers want, and helping the whole community to benefit from the results.

9.13   Since the green paper was published, we have reduced the accounting and audit burden on small parishes. We have done this by raising the threshold below which parishes need only prepare a record of receipts and payments from £5,000 to £50,000. We have announced previously that all parishes that fall clearly below the new threshold can make the changes in the type of accounts kept from 1 April this year. In addition, parishes with budgets below £5,000 annually have, for some time, been able to apply to have their accounts audited only once in three years.

9.14   The Audit Commission recently published a paper 'A New Approach to Local Council Audit', which outlines the new audit regime due to be launched in early 2002 in time for the 2001-02 audit round. This essentially makes the audit process much simpler and therefore much cheaper. Under the new regime, parishes with either receipts or payments of over £100,000 per year will be subject to a 'basic' audit which entails a large amount of self-certification and an analytical review by the auditor based on the paperwork presented. It is estimated that the smallest parishes – below £5,000 – will have audit fees of £30-£50 – a saving of about £100 on the current average cost. Parishes at the £50,000 – £100,000 level will be charged £250 – £350, saving roughly £200 on the average cost. Parishes falling between £100,000 and £500,000 will be subjected to an 'intermediate' audit and should see savings of approximately 12 per cent on current costs. Best value parishes will still be subject to a full audit and may see an increase (about 9 per cent). The Commission's view is that the triennial audit scheme will become redundant under this approach and they estimate that 90 per cent of parishes currently on the triennial scheme should have savings in costs under the new regime.

9.15 We have been exploring the scope for changing the financial regime for the larger parishes. Further details are given at paragraphs 9.30 to 9.32.

Section 137

9.16 Under section 137 (s137) of the Local Government Act 1972, as amended by the Local Government and Housing Act 1989, parishes have a general power to spend up to £3.50 per elector per year on items that are of 'direct benefit' to the area, and where the benefit is 'commensurate with the expenditure to be incurred'. In recent years, more 'headroom' has been created within the £3.50 limit through the introduction of other, specific powers under which parishes can incur expenditure, and the ability for them to exclude s137 expenditure financed by contributions from principal authorities. Although the extent of the s137 power was reduced for principal authorities under the Local Government Act 2000, having been mostly superseded by the new well-being power, it remains relevant in its entirety for parishes.

9.17 A report carried out for the Government by the Aston Business School in 1998 concluded that the s137 arrangements were regarded as

satisfactory by nearly all parishes. But it noted also that the 'headroom' under s137 was reducing rapidly. In addition, there were instances of parishes of various sizes, locations and types saying that the s137 limit had deterred them from spending on additional activities. This was true particularly for some larger and more ambitious parishes. Since then, the annual limit for community councils in Wales has been increased to £5, and two thirds of respondents to the green paper called for the limit to be increased or otherwise amended in England.

9.18 We will legislate therefore to increase the amount of expenditure parishes can incur under s137 to £5 per elector per year. We will then uprate it annually using the Retail Price Index, to avoid the need to revise it continually in future.

Council tax bills

9.19 Details of our plans for reforming the presentation of council tax bills are given in Chapter 6. Although this will not be a statutory requirement, we hope that many billing authorities will show the year on year change in the amount of council tax required by the local parish clearly on the front of the bill.

9.20 In responding to the green paper, some parishes asked for more information on the funding of gross expenditure by principal authorities to be given on council tax bills. This would show that, unlike parishes, they receive revenue support grant and business rates. On balance, we do not believe that further detail of this sort should appear on bills. But we do wish to encourage appropriate and meaningful communication between parishes and their taxpayers in more informal literature. This can include information on sources of parish funding, possibly in a dedicated newsletter.

Double taxation

9.21   Local taxpayers in parished areas can be subject to 'double taxation'. This happens where a service is provided by the parish rather than the principal authority, but the principal authority still charges taxpayers in the parish for the equivalent services it provides elsewhere. It can arise for more than one reason. In a district where a town is unparished, it can happen if the costs of facilities for residents of the unparished town are spread across the council taxpayers of the whole district, rather than being charged only to residents of the town. Double taxation can also happen where a principal authority devolves or transfers a service to a parish, without a corresponding reduction in its share of the council tax bill.

9.22   We are prepared to consider changing legislation if necessary to avoid or minimise double taxation, but not in the immediate future. We would prefer to make the system work better by partnership. We are working with the National Association of Local Councils (NALC) and the Local Government Association to produce some good practice guidance on ways of resolving this issue. We recognise that several possible approaches exist. For example, under the Local Government Finance Act 1992, a district or unitary council may decide to charge only the taxpayers living in those areas where it provides a particular service, rather than sharing the costs between taxpayers in the whole of its area. Alternatively, some principal authorities operate a grant scheme under which they pay parishes a grant towards the costs incurred in providing a service on their behalf. In this case, the principal authority's share of the council tax bill for local payers within the parish is not reduced, but the grant income means that the parish's share of the bill can be kept down. Another approach used occasionally is for a principal authority to transfer a package of services to a parish, including at least one that generates income, such as car parking. The extra income earned can then be used by the parish to offset the costs incurred in providing the other facilities.

Modernising payment authorisation

9.23   Several parishes commented on the requirement under section 150 of the Local Government Act 1972 for every cheque or other order for the payment of money by a parish to be signed by two members of the council. They suggested that this arrangement led to inefficiency and delay. We will speed up the process by making it possible for authorisation to be made using electronic methods, such as by telephone, fax or e-mail.

9.24   We do not propose to go beyond that by, for example, giving officers of parishes the authority to authorise payments. This is because authorisation by two councillors is regarded as a valuable safeguard against fraud. It is important that we do not lose sight of one of the primary objectives of payment systems, which is to prevent the opportunity and reduce the incentive to undertake fraud. We will need to ensure that procedures remain rigorous even as they are speeded up.

Borrowing

9.25   At present, parish borrowing is permitted under the Local Government Act 1972. A ceiling is agreed with the Treasury on the amount of borrowing that parishes will be allowed each year. This amount is £8.5 million for 2001-02, having been £8.0 million in each of the previous two years. The overall level of demand from parishes has also been within, or around, this amount. Over the course of a financial year, DTLR receives about 130 applications for borrowing approval. This represents about 1½ per cent of all parishes. At present, some parishes submit applications when they are not ready to borrow. This may be because they are worried that if they do not apply early, they may not get the approval through by the time they need it, or that the annual total provision might have been fully committed. The result is that some applications are deferred to the following year, creating pressure on the amount of provision available in that financial year.

9.26   Although some green paper responses indicated a preference for a system with no borrowing controls at all, others said that lifting restrictions would be unwise. Many responses suggested however that the present borrowing system for parishes is in need of reform.

9.27   Having considered the green paper responses, we intend to improve the existing borrowing approval system. It operates currently on a first-come, first-served basis with applications assessed against a set of criteria. Applications are first made to the County Associations of NALC, which forward them to NALC's headquarters. NALC acts as an agent for its members and handles much of the administration involved with processing applications, before forwarding them to DTLR for decision. Approval is given as long as the criteria are met, until the total borrowing ceiling is reached, although unused approvals will be recycled to other councils in the queue. We will seek to improve the system by ensuring that there is enough money available for parishes to be confident that they will be able to borrow what they want, when they want, as long as their application meets the criteria. This will be done by dropping the fixed borrowing limit, thus enabling borrowing approval to be given on demand. This arrangement will be kept under

review in case of unexpected changes in the pattern of demand.

9.28   In addition, we will clarify and advertise the criteria more widely, so that parishes can assess readily whether their applications meet the requirements. We will also speed up and streamline the approval process by introducing a standard application form, using electronic processing where available. We will seek to remove one of the tiers of scrutiny from the three-stage process, and be committed to following a timetable for processing applications. These measures should give parishes a clearer, faster process with more certainty. In return, we expect them to submit applications only when they are sure they are ready to borrow.

9.29   We will retain the £500,000 borrowing limit on how much an individual parish can borrow. This is largely to ensure that a handful of large borrowings do not consume too much of the national provision, but it also serves as a simple brake on how much borrowing a parish takes on in any one year. This is a useful control, given the lack of finance expertise and pared down systems in many parishes.

The larger parishes

9.30   Some of the green paper responses have confirmed our belief that the existing system is not well adapted to the needs of the larger parishes. These include the best value parishes.

9.31   We have discussed the issues involved with NALC and representatives of the best value parishes. As a result, we believe that, although the larger parishes should remain within the reformed financial regime for parishes, with spending subject to the s137 limit, those that are subject to best value should – when legislation permits – receive a modest grant from central government. This would bring them more into line with principal authorities, which receive support for best value costs through the revenue support grant system. We envisage that each best value parish would receive a standard amount of £30,000 per year. This is intended to cover audit costs and the corporate costs of carrying out work relating to best value, such as the preparation of performance plans and the management of reviews. The costs of separate best value inspections would continue to be supported through the Audit Commission.

9.32 Details of our plans to give local authorities a general power to charge for discretionary services are given at chapter [8]. More specifically, we propose to use the powers under section 16 of the Local Government Act 1999 to make an order to give local authorities a general power to charge for any discretionary service which they already have powers to provide. The best value parishes will be among the local authorities to receive this power.

CHAPTER 10
Drawing the strands together

10.1   This white paper sets out a route-map for reforming local government finance. In this concluding chapter, we set out how the different reforms work together to meet the nine aims of a good local government finance system, and how they further our broader local government modernisation agenda. We focus, in particular, on promoting local autonomy and partnership working, and how they will need to be underpinned by the work of councillors and by better financial planning and information systems.

Meeting the aims of a good local government finance system

10.2   The aim of **funding all authorities adequately** is partly met by the increases already made in Government grant and support for capital investment. This will now be reinforced by introducing a fairer revenue grant distribution system which puts money where it is most needed and will do most good, rather than replicating past patterns of spend. Our aim of funding all authorities adequately is further enhanced by giving authorities greater freedom on borrowings and local fees and charges, and by the introduction of BIDs.

10.3   Best value and the new comprehensive performance framework outlined in part I of this white paper provide the main means for **promoting continuous improvement in service quality and efficiency**. The local government finance system supports best value by providing adequate funding and by delivering greater predictability and stability. The latter point is particularly important: large and unpredictable changes in grant entitlement could be very damaging to the delivery of best value. The

finance system already provides a financial incentive to improve cost-effectiveness and increase council tax collection rates. We shall eliminate perverse incentives, such as the fire-calls indicator and the deduction of receipts from grant to support capital investment. Above all, local PSAs introduce financial rewards for authorities which meet more stretching targets, introducing into the local government finance system a link between funding and delivery.

10.4   We shall **provide a reasonable degree of predictability and stability** by instituting regular freezes on formula changes and by making floors and ceilings a permanent feature of the revenue grant distribution system. We shall continue with our programme of early release of data used in the grant formulae, and work towards improving upon the timetable. Authorities which have signed local PSAs have been given additional certainty about future levels of grant under the education Standards Fund. We shall deliver greater predictability and stability for taxpayers via fixed revaluation cycles for both business rate and council tax, with transitional relief schemes which would ideally be self-financing. We are encouraging authorities to make firmer forward commitments.

10.5   We shall continue to **support delivery of national priorities and targets** by providing ring-fenced revenue and capital grants, where appropriate. However, our main focus will be on specifying the outcomes and output targets that local authorities and their partners are expected to deliver, giving councils, partnerships and front-line service providers greater freedom to decide how they are met.

10.6   **Giving local authorities real financial freedom and responsibility** is a recurring theme in this white paper. We have already abolished 'crude and universal' capping, and are now committed to abolishing credit approvals and council tax benefit subsidy limitation. We shall give local authorities greater freedom to introduce new fees and charges, and to retain and reinvest the proceeds from fines. Subject to consultation, we shall introduce local discretion on council tax discounts and exemptions. In addition to the financial freedoms which we are extending to all authorities, the new comprehensive performance framework provides a means by which authorities can make a case for additional financial freedoms. But it is important to stress that these freedoms carry new responsibilities with them. In the case of capital investment, authorities become responsible for deciding how much they can prudently afford to borrow. We shall reinforce the responsibility for setting a balanced budget, with adequate reserves, and for living within it.

10.7   There are two main ways in which we shall ensure that the system is **fair to those who use and pay for local authority services**. First, by introducing fairer grant formulae, we shall reduce the disparities in council tax levels and the range of services which authorities are able to provide. Second, we shall take further reserve powers to protect local people from local authority abuse of their powers to determine the level of borrowings. We shall also set conditions on the use of the new fees and charges powers.

10.8   We shall **clarify accountability for financial decisions** by drawing a clearer dividing line between national and local decisions. The Government is accountable for the level of national taxes, including the business rate, and for the capital and revenue grants which these taxes support. Decisions on borrowings, council tax, BIDs, and fees and charges will be taken locally. We shall strengthen and clarify the role of councillors.

10.9   Making the system **intelligible and transparent to all stakeholders** will be one of the key aims in the design of the new grant formulae. Chapter 2 explains how governors,

teachers and parents can track the financial decisions that lead to the setting of the budget for their school.

10.10 We have already acted to **facilitate partnership working** by eliminating the obstacles to pooling of budgets. Greater predictability and stability of funding makes it easier for authorities to enter into longer-term contractual commitments with partners. BIDs pave the way for a more constructive relationship between councils and local businesses. In extending local PSAs to all upper tier authorities, we shall encourage joint proposals from counties and their district councils, as well as the involvement of other local partners in delivering PSA targets.

10.11 We **encourage consultation** on capital investment plans (chapter 4), on budget and council tax increases (chapter 6) and fees and charges (chapter 8). Chapter 7 deals with referenda on BIDs.

Promoting local autonomy and financial responsibility

10.12 Promoting local autonomy is a central goal of the local government modernisation agenda. Financial autonomy is an important component of this. Local authorities will have little credibility with their own voters and with local partners if they do not have sufficient financial freedom of manoeuvre to fund local spending priorities, to support local solutions and to enter into long-term financial commitments with partners. Under this white paper, the Government will extend a large number of new financial freedoms and responsibilities to local authorities – summarised at paragraph 10.6. However, promoting local autonomy also requires actions and changes of attitude on the part of local authorities.

10.13 Increased financial freedom brings with it increased financial responsibility. And good financial management is one of the keys to successful service delivery. This is why the Government intends to ensure that the Audit Commission's comprehensive performance assessment takes proper account of an authority's financial performance. Chapter 6 in part one of the white paper identifies a number of issues and actions that are important for sound financial management. The remainder of this chapter discusses these in greater detail.

SETTING THE BUDGET

10.14 Local authorities have an underlying responsibility to promote the interests of their taxpayers and their communities. Lobbying for additional funding is a facet of this. It is a legitimate and important activity, but it needs careful handling. For the present financial year, the average general grant increase was 4½ per cent and the average total grant increase was over 7 per cent. There are cases of authorities, which secured grant increases in line with the national average, but still maintained publicly that they were faced with a choice between steep council tax increases and budget cuts. Such a claim is not plausible. It undermines the authority's credibility with Government and – more importantly – with its own voters.

10.15 A local authority should be able to offset increases in input costs by improvements in cost-effectiveness. Local authority input costs have risen broadly in line with inflation in recent years, i.e. by 2–2½ per cent a year. Across the economy as a whole, public and private sector bodies have improved productivity by the same 2–2½ per cent a year, and there is no reason why local authorities should not match this. So, even an authority that gets a floor increase in grant should be budgeting for improvements and increases in the services it provides, not for cuts.

10.16 The real problem for local authorities is that the demands made on them are also increasing. It is not a question of cuts, but it is a question of how many of these demands the authority can accommodate. Like any other body in the public, private or voluntary sectors, local authority budget-setting involves setting priorities and making choices. However hard the authority may have fought for increased funding, it is important that it accepts responsibility for making and defending these budget choices.

10.17 The existing legislation requires local authorities to set a balanced budget. In setting the budget, they are required to consider contingencies and the need for reserves. It is normal practice for authorities to have earmarked reserves to cover specific risks, plus a general reserve to cover unforeseen costs. It is obviously important that authorities look at their reserves in the round, and take account of factors such as the extent of their insurance cover and the risks they bear on major capital investment projects. However, the existing legislation does not require authorities to maintain reserves. CIPFA issued a paper on budgeting for reserves in 1995, but this has no formal status.

10.18 Authorities need to ensure that they budget for sufficient reserves to cover all significant identified risks and a reasonable allowance for those unidentified. Primarily this is an obligation for them to deal with themselves as part of the budget process. But we propose to take a series of measures to give it added weight. We welcome the work CIPFA is doing on the role of the chief finance officer in local government. We shall invite CIPFA to take account of this white paper's proposals in that work, so that up-to-date professional guidance is available on reserves. In addition we shall legislate to place a new statutory duty on the chief finance officer to report to the authority, at the time the council tax is set, on the robustness of the budget calculations and the adequacy of the reserves. This will be a public report.

10.19 Our hope is that these measures will be sufficient to ensure that all authorities budget for an adequate level of reserves. We recognise that some authorities will need time to achieve an adequate level. However, we shall also take powers to enable the Secretary of State to specify in regulations a statutory minimum level of reserves for which authorities must provide in their budgets. Our preference would be not to make use of these powers, but we should not hesitate to do so if it emerged that authorities were failing to remedy deficiencies or were running down reserves against the advice of their finance officers. We should consult local government about the level at which the statutory minimum would be set.

MONITORING SPEND

10.20 We shall legislate to create a new duty on local authorities to keep their finances under review during the year, and to take corrective action if there is evidence that financial pressures will result in a budget overspend. In most cases, this action will involve reducing costs, increasing fees and charges, or drawing on reserves.

10.21 In the most serious cases, where budget problems are forecast to exhaust all the resources available to an authority, existing legislation requires the chief finance officer to issue a formal report to the council. This report must be considered by the council within 21 days, and until it is considered the council is prohibited from entering into new agreements involving expenditure. We see this as a valuable safeguard, and we intend that it should remain. The new duty proposed in the previous paragraph is complementary to it. However, recent

experience of the issue of such a report has indicated that the temporary ban on new agreements can delay essential corrective action. We therefore intend to legislate to exempt from the prohibition agreements essential to deal with the overspend or to prevent its recurrence. Exemption would be conditional on the chief finance officer certifying in each case that these criteria had been met.

10.22 Local authorities do not have the power to increase their council tax during the year. We have concluded, on balance, that they should not acquire such a power. However, this reinforces the need to keep a close watch on revenue and capital spend during the year. Scrutiny committees have a key role to play here – see paragraph 10.40.

DEALING WITH UNFORESEEN SPENDING PRESSURES

10.23 Local authorities must have the capacity to deal with unforeseen spending pressures. Over the last 12 months, many authorities have incurred additional costs dealing with flooding or foot-and-mouth disease, and many have also found that their expenditure on social services has exceeded their budget provision. In addition, individual authorities face purely local spending pressures, often arising from capital projects which they have undertaken or underwritten, or from legal actions. Paragraph 10.17 deals with the need for adequate reserves. But, in order to decide what provision to make for such pressures, authorities need to know what help they can expect from Government.

10.24 In cases where the problem arises from circumstances beyond the authority's own control, Government help will take the form of further grant. The Bellwin scheme is the main vehicle for this, although the Government can also provide financial support in other ways, e.g.

ring-fenced grant for authorities providing hardship relief on business rates to firms affected by foot-and-mouth. We have been reviewing the working of the Bellwin scheme with local government, and will consult on funding arrangements for the scheme.

10.25 The Government endorses the recommendations of the review group, which are as follows. We should continue to limit the scheme to costs incurred by local authorities in dealing with emergencies or disasters which threaten life or property. All schemes of financial assistance will require the local authority to make a financial contribution, and the review group considered that the existing threshold at which Bellwin grants begin to contribute to the cost of dealing with an emergency (0.2 per cent of an authority's budget) and the proportion they fund (usually 85 per cent of marginal costs above this level) represent an appropriate balance between local and central responsibility. We should consider the possibility of a more flexible approach on some short-term capital expenditure, where this would represent good value for money. However, we should continue to exclude costs which are insurable, since we do not believe it is sensible to subsidise authorities to under-insure. In the interests of simplicity, eligibility for Bellwin grant to cover minimum insurance excesses should be removed. We should retain on a permanent basis all the administrative improvements introduced recently. We should set the funding of the Bellwin scheme on a proper footing by introducing new funding arrangements, with separate provision earmarked for Bellwin expenditure which could be carried forward if not used. The Government has now decided to take the legislative steps necessary to make combined fire authorities (CFAs) major precepting authorities (see chapter 6). In line with this, the Government will legislate to enable CFAs to apply directly for assistance under the Bellwin scheme.

10.26 The Government is also prepared to help in cases where the authority bears some or all of the responsibility for the funding problem. The financial situation in the London Borough of Hackney is the most recent case. However, it is important to stress two points. First, such assistance is very much a last resort, and will not be provided unless the Government is satisfied that all other options have been exhausted. Second, the assistance does not currently result in any increase in grant from Government. Under the existing capital finance system, the assistance takes the form of unsupported credit approvals, which allow the authority to borrow additional funds, but the cost of repaying these borrowings is borne by the authority and its taxpayers. Under the new capital finance regime the Government would be prepared to facilitate the use of unsupported borrowing by an authority to cover a revenue shortfall. But we would not wish such borrowing to take the authority above its prudential borrowing limit. So in extreme cases it might be necessary to give grant assistance. But authorities should expect such assistance to be accompanied by the use of other powers of intervention and control, such as the reserve power to limit the authority's future borrowing ability and powers under the best value legislation.

PROVIDING FINANCIAL INFORMATION

10.27 Modernising the local government finance system requires rapid access to relevant and accurate financial information. We shall move towards the electronic collection and dissemination of local government finance statistics, and we shall make data available on the internet as soon as it has been validated. This will include the data on authorities' budget and council tax increases. Alongside improvements in access to electronic data, we will be reviewing the local government financial statistics publication for 2002. We will continue with our program of early release of data used in the grant formulae, and work towards improving upon the timetable. Starting this year, electronic dissemination will be our main means of communicating information on local authorities' general grant entitlements.

10.28 The existing regulations require local authorities' annual accounts to be prepared and approved within six months of the end of the financial year (i.e. by 30 September) and to be published within a further three months (i.e. by 31 December). This is a relaxed timetable, compared with private sector companies and other bodies. As indicated in part one, the Government intends to align the date for the preparation and approval of the accounts with the date for the publication of the best value performance plan (30 June). The date for the publication of the accounts will also be brought forward.

10.29 An authority's audited accounts are important, because they provide a comprehensive and authoritative statement of its assets and liabilities, as well as its income and spending. However, there are some more challenging information requirements within the new local government finance system. The financial information produced within the authority to allow members to monitor spend must be accurate and timely. Members will need a lot of technical information, presented in a manner which is comprehensible to non-experts, to help them determine prudent levels of borrowing and reserves. Consultation with local people and partners makes even more serious demands on the ability of finance officers to compress a lot of data on revenue and spending plans into a meaningful set of choices.

PLANNING AHEAD

10.30 The best councils already look beyond the immediate future in their financial planning. Their medium term revenue and capital budgets are driven by a clear vision of the future for their area and a realistic strategy for getting there. Their budgets link the resources employed with the outcomes they intend to achieve. They accept uncertainty as a fact of life and make allowances for it in their planning processes.

10.31 The new prudential system will bring added urgency to all authorities adopting these practices. Affordability is at the heart of the new system. Authorities undertaking borrowing without Government support must be confident that they can finance the repayments without putting future services in jeopardy. The process of preparing revenue forecasts for the medium term will identify the trends in income and expenditure into which the repayments will need to be absorbed. This must be accompanied by an assessment of risks affecting the forecasts, which will enable authorities to judge how far they can make use of apparent headroom in future years' budgets. To be useful these forecasts must look at least three years ahead, but authorities will also need to be alert to developments beyond that horizon that might affect the affordability of borrowing.

WORKING IN PARTNERSHIP

10.32 As well as promoting local autonomy, the modernisation agenda also stresses the need for partnership working. The two goals are not inconsistent. In the interests of accountability, it must be clear who is responsible for local financial decisions. In the case of BIDs, businesses have the final say on whether or not an additional rate is levied. Local authorities have the final say on how their budgets are allocated and spent, and are answerable to local people for the council tax and charges they set. But this is not an obstacle to consultation or partnership working.

10.33 At various points in this paper, we have touched on the need for proper consultation with local people on financial issues. We do not intend to legislate on the circumstances in which an authority should consult or how it should establish local views. That is a matter for the political judgement of authorities. But they may well wish to integrate these consultation exercises with one another and with the existing requirements to consult on the best value performance plan and the community strategy. This allows voters to make informed long-term judgements about the level of taxes and charges the authority proposes alongside the investments and service improvements they will support. It also allows business to decide whether or not to back a BID to deliver additional initiatives which cannot be funded in the proposed core budget for future years. However and whenever it is conducted, the consultation exercise will inform council decisions, not determine them.

10.34 The local strategic partnership's views on the neighbourhood renewal strategy will be essential and will inform the authority's decisions on how to spend its NRF grant. NRF is a targeted grant, providing additional resources for local authorities to improve mainstream services in the most deprived areas, including contributing to the achievement of the floor targets to narrow the gap between deprived areas and the rest of the country. It can be spent in any way that will tackle deprivation in the most deprived neighbourhoods and can support services provided by the local authority, by members of the local strategic partnership and by others. Local authorities have been encouraged to consult local strategic partnerships on the allocation of NRF grant.

10.35 We are satisfied that there are no legal obstacles to budget pooling. A county council, district council, police or fire authority and health authority may all pool budgets with one another to secure joint objectives. Paragraph 10.4 summarises the steps we are taking to ensure that local authorities can predict their future grant entitlement with a greater degree of confidence. It is essential that local authorities extend the benefits of financial predictability and stability to their own budget-holders, particularly to schools and other front-line service-providers. But it also allows them to enter into longer-term financial commitments to external partners. This is particularly valuable to voluntary sector bodies.

10.36 The boundary-line between services provided in-house and services contracted-out will shift constantly as a result of best value reviews. For some services, there will be a move to long-term partnership agreements with private sector suppliers, replacing short-term service contracts. There are many services where joint procurement or joint delivery has obvious scope to secure economies of scale, as well as providing users with a more seamless service. In addition to joint delivery or procurement of their council tax billing services, district councils will need to look at the benefits of combining service provision of business rate billing, council tax and housing benefit payments, and other billing and payments work. Greater certainty about future funding facilitates sound long-term decisions. The local government finance system offers incentives to authorities to cut costs. And the greater freedom and responsibility provided for in this white paper should make authorities more sensitive to the case for sharing or transferring risk, particularly in relation to capital projects.

THE ROLE OF OFFICERS

10.37 Sound finance in local government depends on good quality advice and effective management by officers. The chief finance officer has an especially important role to play in providing professional advice on financial issues and maintaining a strategic overview of an authority's financial situation. This role will be enhanced by the responsibility to advise on the use of the new borrowing and charging freedoms and by the new duty to report on budgets and reserves when the council tax is set. But in a well-run authority all officers take responsibility for the finances of the services they manage. Financial management is integrated with the management of the services, so that financial resources can be used with maximum effectiveness and all take responsibility for the resources they are consuming. The proposals in this paper should also help these other officers in fulfilling their roles. The borrowing and charging freedoms will broaden the range of options open to them in financing services, and service planning will be assisted by the new emphasis placed on preparing medium term revenue and capital budgets.

THE ROLE OF COUNCILLORS

10.38 Traditionally, the main input from councillors has been to the setting of the authority's annual budget. This will remain a key role, because striking the right balance between council tax and service levels is a political decision. So is the setting of a prudent level of reserves. Under new executive arrangements the executive of the local authority will take the lead in framing proposals. However, there is an important role for all councillors in scrutinising the budgets that come before them, as responsibility for approving the annual budget remains a function of the full council. They

need to be satisfied that the budget distinguishes clearly between increases in input costs, savings resulting from improved efficiency, increases or decreases in demand, and the cost of new initiatives and services. They also need to satisfy themselves that budgets are consistent with the best value performance plan and the outcomes of best value reviews, and that the allocation of budgets is fair.

10.39 However, the white paper increases local authority freedom and responsibility in many areas, and it is important that the freedom is exercised by councillors, since the responsibility clearly rests with them. The decision on how much the authority can prudently borrow (see chapter 4) is a particularly important case in point. It will reflect advice from officers, taking into account the CIPFA Code, but the decision is one for the full council. It is important that members own this decision, and understand the risks involved in the capital investment programme.

10.40 Paragraph 10.20 refers to the new duty to keep finances under review and to take corrective action to avert a potential budget overspend. This will be a duty on authorities. The aim is to ensure that members take the lead in monitoring the financial performance of the authority, as well as its delivery of services. Scrutiny committees in particular have a lead role here. Monitoring should cover capital investment as well as revenue spend. Like other public sector bodies, local authorities spend a very high proportion of their capital budgets in the last quarter of the financial year – across England, the average is 45 per cent. One source of this problem, which we are remedying, has been late decisions by Government. However, authorities also need to check that their own internal authorisation procedures are not causing delay.

10.41 Last but not least, it must be for members to decide when and how to consult local people and partners on the authority's budget for the coming year or its longer-term spending and revenue-raising plans.

10.42 All but the smallest authorities are currently implementing the new executive arrangements provided for in the Local Government Act 2000. The new structures make explicit provision for the handling of the key financial decisions of the Council. Properly implemented they provide for a dynamic process of decision making, debate and review, involving executive, full council and overview and scrutiny committees, that should open up financial issues for examination and lead to sound and well founded decisions. The overview and scrutiny committees have particularly important roles to play. They should be questioning the plans of the executive, scrutinising performance against budget, and reviewing the delivery and cost effectiveness of all the authority's activities. They should aim to use their powers to promote the effective use of financial resources to meet the needs of their community and ensure the financial stability of the council.

Conclusion

10.43 This white paper offers substantial new financial freedoms to local authorities. But the benefits of the new freedoms will not be fully realised unless members and officers grasp the opportunities they offer and make imaginative use of them for the benefit of the people they serve. New fields of decision making will be opened up which were previously closed off by statutory constraints. Authorities will need to decide how they want to use these freedoms, consulting their communities. They will need to work with and, where appropriate, pool resources with other partners. Sound and transparent financial management systems and decision making processes are essential underpinning if authorities are to exercise their increased responsibilities effectively and deliver the high quality services that they and their communities wish to see.